To Judy. Magness

Civil Rights Brothers

Allan Ward.

Other Books by Allan Ward

Beyond the Visible Spectrum

Postmodern Zen: a path of paradox and process

Lucian (a novel)

Trickster (a novel)

The Rhubarb Club: Recollections and Recipes

Golden Thunder: A Quest for the Inner Poet

LifeQuest Poets: A Journey of Discovery and Sharing

Civil Rights Brothers

The Journey of
Albert Porter and Allan Ward

Allan Ward

Award Press
6609 Sherry Drive
Little Rock, AR 72204
alward@ualr.edu

ISBN: 978-0-9748636-7-2

Copyeditor: Kevin Jones
Design: H. K. Stewart
Cover photograph: courtesy of Fay Royce

Printed in the United States of America

This book is printed on archival-quality paper that meets requirements of the American National Standard for Information Sciences, Permanence of Paper, Printed Library Materials, ANSI Z39.48-1984.

The good neighbor looks beyond the external accidents and discerns those inner qualities that make all men human and, therefore, brothers.

—Martin Luther King, Jr.

1

When I was a student at the University of Arizona, I watched a Native American artist making a ring of silver, turquoise, and coral, with a design on the side. I asked about its meaning. The artist told me it was a Native American sign language symbol for friendship. It had a mound representing a mountain, with a line on either side of the mountain. These, he said, represented two people starting out in two different places, far apart, separated by the mountain, unknown to one another. But the lines moved closer to each other along the base of the mountain, until they came together, and then side by side, they continued on next to each other. This, he explained, was the sign for friendship: two who meet and continue the journey together.

When I met Albert Porter, that symbol came to mind. We had grown up in different places in the country, but when circumstances brought us together, our paths became parallel. Coming in the time and place that our meeting occurred—the Civil Rights 60s in the South—people saw it as an unusual friendship. Outwardly they saw what they would refer to as a black man and a white man working together. What they could not see was that inwardly we were more alike than anyone else either of us had ever met. Many have asked us how such cooperation in the civil rights movement and for other social causes came about and have requested that the story be written. Responding to those requests, this is that story.

2

Symbolically on opposite sides of the mountain, Albert grew up in McComb, a small town in Mississippi, and I grew up in Bellwood, Illinois, a suburb of Chicago. Early on, he developed a passion for equality of everyone and the removal of barriers to opportunities. He credited this, in part, to his grandmother's repeated reminder that "no one is any better than you, and you are no better than anyone else." He began as a youth to participate in activities supporting civil rights activities.

At the same time, I was distressed as a child to see people behave toward others in hurtful ways. When I was in sixth grade, one Sunday morning, a black man came to enter the segregated church my family attended. I saw the adults curse and threaten him and refuse him entry.

There went through my mind the Biblical phrase that "whatsoever you do to the least of these, my brethren, do ye also unto me," which meant to me that they had just locked goodness out of the church. If goodness was not there, I felt I could not return but somehow must help such behavior to cease and instead help create equality for all. I wanted to dedicate myself to helping interracial interaction and understanding in whatever way I could.

I felt confused that this sense of equality seemed so apparent to me when the adults in my environment felt otherwise. My concerned parents took me to our family doctor to see if he could diagnose what my problem was. He suggested to them to let me follow my own course.

I went to my minister and poured out my heart-felt concerns. He said that treating everyone as equals might seem like a good idea, but when it came to race-mixing, we just had to compromise.

In 1952 I was a senior in high school when we had class photos taken. We exchanged the small pictures with our friends, and I took all those I had received and laid them out on my study desk at home. My father, looking at them, reached over, picked up the one of a black classmate, tore it up, and said I was never to bring a photo like that into the house again. I felt sorry that my parents had such attitudes and wondered why I saw things so differently.

Throughout college, I explored ways to help integration. When in 1960 I finished my Ph.D. degree in communication at Ohio University, the civil rights activities were daily news. I wanted to get in the middle of the movement and use my major in communications to find ways to bring people together. I wanted to seek ways for us to see each other as real, individual human beings and not as categories.

Albert served in the military, being present at the Normandy invasion in June 1944. When he returned to

Mississippi, he wanted to major in accounting, but no state school for African Americans offered the degree. Old Miss had it, but he was not permitted there. To avoid the issue, Mississippi would pay his way to any school in the country that offered the degree. So he went not only to a series of different campuses but also different states, taking courses in Florida, Kentucky, Michigan, Oregon, Washington, and California.

After finishing his schooling, he took a faculty and administrative position at Saints Junior college in Lexington, Mississippi. It was there that he met and married another faculty member, Fanye Ranger. Being from Texas, she joked about being a Texas Ranger. His outstanding work there came to the attention of Lane College in Jackson, Tennessee. He was offered a job as business manager at Lane in 1958.

The students at Lane wanted to participate in the demonstrations and sit-ins in Jackson, and the college president said they could if they had a faculty advisor. They went through the staff asking, but no one agreed to get involved until they asked Albert. He said yes and began to train them in the peaceful resistance advocated by Martin Luther King, Jr.

Meanwhile, in 1960, I was finishing my degree in Ohio and exploring the possibilities of getting a teaching job in the South so I could help in civil rights activities. It soon became obvious I could not get a job at a white state institution and participate in the civil rights activities. I received an offer from a black state school, until they asked for my photo, and after it had arrived, the dean wrote a poignant letter saying if they hired me, the state would close their school the next day. He added that he hoped a day could come when people like himself and me could actually meet and even go to a restaurant together.

My African-American friends at Ohio University told me that while they respected my intentions of heading south to work with civil rights, they would never see me again, since, being from the north where it was bad enough, they would never go below the Mason-Dixon Line.

But while I was away from campus at a conference, they met together and decided that the only place I could get a job was at a private African-American college. They contacted multiple institutions on my behalf, and when I returned to campus, they informed me they had found a teaching position for me at Lane College in Jackson, Tennessee.

3

In August 1960, I moved into a faculty apartment on the Lane campus. After getting my classes started, I was ready to find out who was leading the civil rights activities so I could be included.

Symbolically, as in the Native-American design, Albert and I had now come around from our opposite sides of the mountain and were in the same time and place.

One evening at a gathering in another faculty apartment, I asked the host to tell me who was leading the civil rights activities. He pointed across the room to Albert.

I went over and expressed my wish to be of service in any way possible, especially to bring people together for discussions. He said we could start immediately.

Albert explained there were two white private denominational colleges in the city. He had just received a call from the wife of a faculty member at one of them, saying that several of the faculty wives were concerned about the upset to the city caused by the demonstrations, and asked him, as leader of the demonstrations, to come to her home after dark to talk to the ladies. Albert had asked a female faculty member at Lane to accompany him, and now, he said, I could come too, perhaps "helping to act as a buffer."

When darkness descended, the three of us drove to the woman's home. The hostess stood at the door motioning us to hurry in, looking up and down the street. "Were you followed?" she asked. She said she feared shootings or bombings if it was discovered that this meeting was taking place. She closed the door, pulled down the shades, and ushered us into the circle of women.

Why just women? She explained that if the men had attended, and the college discovered they had been at such a meeting, they would immediately have been fired. So the men were all out in other places establishing alibis. Should the meeting be discovered, they and their wives had agreed that the men would draw upon another stereotype with a dismissive, *"Oh, you know how women are."*

The teacups handed out by the hostess rattled like an orchestra of dishes in the hands of the nervous women. "Why are you destroying our city?" blurted out one lady. Albert gently and kindly explained the demonstrations were to open up equal opportunities for all of the children. One of the ladies exclaimed, "What? You mean you love your children, too?"

The reference to children opened the door for a conversation of individuals. Some of the participants indicated that this was the first time in their lives they had ever had a conversation with a black person, other than giving instructions to yard men and cleaning women.

When they finally asked what they could do to help the city, Albert explained that we needed this discussion group to continue so we could talk on an ongoing basis, coming to know and trust each other. Also we should identify other people to bring together to form additional interracial discussion groups.

The marvel of communication was working, and over the following months we formed many groups, keeping them relatively small so participants could express themselves and come to know those in their group. It was all done quietly with no publicity, and Albert and I were the coordinators at each of these groups. These efforts occupied our time on many nights after our workdays ended.

4

There were other evening activities as well. Training with the students continued to prepare them to respond peaceably to what they might encounter during the sit-ins and demonstrations. At our practice sessions, with some of the students seated on chairs at a table, simulating their being at a lunch counter during a sit-in, other students would play the roles of antagonists, hurling curses and epithets at them, throwing water in their faces, and pushing them off the chairs.

The students themselves came with a variety of previous experiences and stories. One of them had been jailed, raped by a jailer, and conceived a child. She felt the life that had been created, even under such terrible circumstances, was innocent and deserved to live. She gave birth, raising the child as a single mother while pursuing her education.

We also met with the adult African Americans in the community to keep them posted on what was being done. When students were jailed, we arranged to get them released. Between the interracial discussion groups and the planning and training meetings, almost every evening was taken.

= = =

Another kind of activity that occupied some of the evenings was the literacy training. Martin Luther King, Jr., wanted to help adults who had never received the opportunity to learn to read and write. Groups across the South formed local programs to take volunteers to the illiterate who wanted help. In Jackson, Albert and I found several other volunteers, all African Americans. A carload of us headed out once a week to the rural areas, found our way to houses where an eager adult, often in advanced years, waited for us.

At each stop, one of us went into the home to teach, and the car drove on to drop off the next and the next, until the driver found the last home on the route. When the driver finished with his trainee, he retraced his route and picked up all of the rest of us. We speculated on what might occur on the night roads we traveled if local authorities knew what we were doing. One evening in a rural community, a police car followed us all the way to the main road and then turned around without stopping us.

I was paired with a farmer in his 70s who had longed to learn to read and write, especially to read newspapers. Finally he had his chance to try. I sat at the kitchen table with him, and the whole family gathered around. We traced letters of the alphabet, we sounded them, we assembled letters into words and pronounced them, and we built words into sentences. Gradually, week by week, his ability grew.

Many sessions into our being together, my farmer grinned at me when I entered the farmhouse. He picked up the newspaper and began to read slowly and carefully an article with which he had been practicing to display his achievement.

Then he reached over the table and took my hands and told me, "You are the first white person to ever be in this house and the first I have ever been able to talk with," as tears rolled down his cheeks.

= = =

Not only were Albert and I together every evening at these various activities, but on the weekends as well. The civil rights leaders in towns across the South kept in touch, letting each other know of projects being planned that welcomed help from other communities.

So when one area had plans to do voter registration, we all knew they would welcome additional volunteers from out of town. So after work on Friday afternoons, Albert and I would often head out of town to drive to Atlanta or Birmingham or New Orleans or Jacksonville, often driving most of the night. On Saturday, the assembled volunteers would receive directives to get to their sections of town. Then we walked up and down the streets, house to house, to talk with the occupants to see if they were registered to vote, and if not, to make it possible for them to do so.

On answering their doors, the occupants would look strangely at me. Albert would have to assure them that I was all right and wanted to support voter registration. I was dependent on his validation to be accepted rather than suspected.

The volunteers would meet back together in the evening to share our results and plan for more home visits on Sunday along with visits to church congregations. Then on Sunday night Albert and I would drive back to Jackson.

We had time on these drives, weekend after weekend, to talk about all the activities we were experiencing. And we would experiment to see where changes were taking place. In one drive from Tennessee to Florida, we stopped in every town at many hotels and motels along the route to see if we could get a room for the night.

I would go alone into the white motels, and Albert would go alone into the black motels. In each case we would ask if they had a room for two. If they said yes, then as one of us would start to register, he would explain the race of the other one out in the car. Suddenly the manager would discover that all the rooms were taken, and they had no place for us.

This happened at dozens of places all the way to Florida. Finally at one black motel, the manager said we could have a room, but I would have to cover up and rush into the room so no one could see me, and we would have to leave before sunrise. He said that if I was seen there, the place might be bombed by segregationists. So we rested briefly, exited before the dawn, and drove on.

We had similar adventures in getting food along the way. The events were like an ongoing sociological adventure, with our never-ending conversations about the meaning of the behaviors we encountered and how we could accelerate the process of change.

For black families traveling, with relatively few places to stop, some African-American funeral parlors opened their facilities for overnight stays. Visitors often slept on surfaces usually used for other purposes.

5

Back in Jackson, Albert received a phone call from a local white man who said it was urgent that they talk, but it had to be at night after dark so he would not be seen coming to Albert's house. He arrived in the darkness and hurried inside.

The man had been in a meeting with city officials. Although in such gatherings he felt he could say little about his personal approval of integration lest he be excluded from such gatherings, he felt deeply the injustice of segregation.

At the meeting that day, he explained, a major city official "put a price" on Albert's head. The official was not planning to announce it to the general public, but to spread the word on the streets, hoping some "homeless drunk" would kill Albert and seek to collect the reward. The city official meanwhile could remain distanced from the deed.

The man, with deep emotions, warned Albert to never let his wife drive anywhere alone in the car, or they might try to kill her, too. Also, he said, never let your children play outside in your yard, or drive-by shooters might try to kill them.

Even though the college students had not heard this specific information, they reasoned that Albert, as recognized leader of the movement, was in growing danger. On their own, they set up all-night watches of his home, each taking an hour or two at a time, to at least sound an alarm if they saw something suspicious, hoping such a warning might provide a few moments escape time from bombs or bullets.

= = =

On a weekend when Albert planned to drive to McComb, Mississippi, to see his parents, he asked me to come along. When we crossed the line into Mississippi, he reminded me that we could be stopped by the police for driving in the front seat together.

Arriving at his home, his mother welcomed me, but his father went into another room, pacing and mumbling about all of us being arrested. He explained that it was against the law for black and white people to be in the same house socially in the evening. His father was visibly shaking with fear, unable to steady himself.

Albert explained to his folks that wherever one of us went, the other was welcome to come also, and that if there was to be social change, it had to start with simple events, like traveling and staying together. Gradually his father calmed down, returned from the back room, and we all sat down to supper at the kitchen table together.

= = =

It was not the same with my parents. They had come to the graduation ceremony in Ohio when I received my

Ph.D. They were happy at first to know I had a job teaching at a college in Tennessee, until I told them it was an African-American school. They were not just shocked, but my mother said that if I did this, it would have been better if I had never been born.

Under no circumstances would they even consider visiting me in Tennessee. They agreed that I could come to visit them in Albuquerque, the city to which they had retired. However they said I must never tell any of their friends the true nature of the school or of my civil rights activities, fearing that if I did, their friends would never associate with them again. I honored their wishes.

= = =

Also in Ohio, at the time I was receiving my degree, one of my faculty advisors, with whom I had enjoyed a pleasant relationship up until that time, called me into his office when he found out where I was going to teach. He said, "If we had known you were going to waste your degree like this, we should never have wasted our time on you, or money for your teaching fellowship."

In Jackson, I was contacted by the Ohio University alumni magazine asking me to write an article about what it was like being "a white teacher at a black college." After it was printed, I returned to campus for a homecoming.

To my surprise, my faculty advisor who had considered my use of the degree to be "a waste" found me and asked me to come to his office. There, he said he realized now that I was using my communication training in its most important way, to help bring real people together to communicate and work out real problems. Then, as his eyes teared, he said, "If I had the guts, I would do the same thing as you, but I don't."

6

In the spring of 1964, Albert was walking with the students carrying signs on a downtown Jackson sidewalk that urged stores to hire black clerks. The African-American population was refraining from purchasing anything at those stores until hiring changes were made.

White people cursed the demonstrators as they passed by. One man came out of the crowd, pulled a pistol from his pocket, walked up to Albert, held the gun to Albert's head, and in a rush of racial slurs and epithets, shouted that he was going to "blow your brains out."

Albert never flinched nor stopped walking, carrying his sign urging equal hiring opportunity for all. The man walked beside him, pushing the barrel of the gun harder against his head, repeating what he was going to do.

Albert said calmly, "You do what you think is best, and I must do what I think is best," and continued walking. This reaction was apparently so contrary to what the man expected that he began to tremble and babble and, waving the gun in the air, went running off into the crowd.

Later that day, as word of the incident spread around campus and in the African-American community, people were saying very negative things about the would-be assassin. When Albert heard these things, he would gently explain to them that they must respect that man's sincerity. The man was sincerely doing what he thought was right, Albert said, and when that man gained insight into the rightness of equality, he would be equally sincere about that. We must respect and encourage the positive virtues of everyone.

This became an ongoing practice that Albert and I had in our extended conversations, looking for the positive qualities in people and seeking to identify them, and encouraging others to do likewise.

= = =

Looking for positive qualities in others became part of our gatherings to promote interracial discussions. As word spread of what we were doing with ongoing interracial discussion groups in Jackson, we were being invited to travel on weekends to Mississippi, Alabama, Louisiana, Georgia, the Carolinas, and other states to help establish groups there.

As transitions in attitudes, customs, and laws were taking place, it was not possible to anticipate at any given time in any given location just what local reactions would be. A big part of that uncertainty was related to what the attitude of local law enforcement officers would be.

In a city in Georgia, at an interracial meeting in the African-American host's apartment, our discussion was interrupted by loud thuds of things hitting the outside walls. The apartment entrance was in an alleyway, just off the street. Looking out the window, we saw that a white mob had gathered, throwing bricks and stones against the wall of the building.

Seeing us at the window, the crowd shouted their worst threat—that they were calling the police to come and "get" us. Later, when the mob sounds abated, we looked out again. The police had been called and had arrived, but to the mob's surprise had moved the crowd from the alley back to the street. When we went to the door leading into the alley, the police shouted at us, saying they were not going to try to control the mob, and to get out of there. Several in our group rushed out, running the other way down the alley. The police shrugged, walked away, and let the mob chase after the runners.

The rest of us stayed inside the apartment until the crowd was gone, and then left after dark. We learned later that those of our group who had run down the alley had gotten to their cars and had all escaped safely.

7

Even as new laws were passed, it was unpredictable how individuals would respond. Even though busses were technically integrated, allowing people to sit in any available seat, front or back, the old practice of whites in front and blacks in back did not change overnight.

One weekend when I had traveled by bus to a distant city and was ready to return on Sunday night, I realized when I got on the coach that something was amiss. Everyone on the bus was white except for one African American sitting in the mid-section in a window seat. Although there were people standing in the aisle, no one would sit beside him.

Since the process of social change is a matter of doing the simple and ordinary in regards to everyone, I moved down the aisle and sat in the empty seat. A murmur filled the bus. I spoke to the man in a simple and ordinary exchange one might have on meeting a new person on a bus, asking him about where he had gotten on and how far he was going.

He looked surprised, and the standing passengers huddled in closer to us, apparently trying to hear what we were saying. I had an all-night ride ahead of me, and he was going further still. The conversation that started with those simple questions continued through all hours of the night. He expressed surprise when I told him where I worked. He asked detailed questions about my experiences there and about my civil rights involvement.

As dawn came, I shook his hand as I got off the bus and walked more than a mile from the bus station to the college campus, straight to the room for my first class, without benefit of any sleep all night.

Days passed. One morning, as I walked through the central campus building to go down the corridor to the room for my first class, I saw a familiar face, the rider on the bus. He smiled, "Thought you'd stand out, and I wouldn't have any trouble finding you."

Then he said he came to tell me the context of that nighttime bus journey we had unexpectedly shared together. He explained that he had been working in civil rights activities, along with others following closely the non-violent concept and methods of Dr. Martin Luther King, Jr. But people who ridiculed King's philosophy and espoused militance and violence had gotten to him, reached his emotions, and wanted him to join them. They taunted him, asking if he had ever met one white man who was "all right." He admitted no, and that had been the tipping point. He left the King projects and took the bus to join a militant group advocating separation and violence. That had been the night of our journey together. He said that, after our conversation, when he got off the bus at his destination, he went straight to the counter, bought a ticket on the next bus to return home, and continued his efforts with King's group. And he said thank you as we embraced.

= = =

Movie theaters had been segregated. Since I went to no theaters, restaurants, or other public places if they were unavailable to everyone, I saw virtually no films for years. With ongoing demonstrations and negotiations, different venues would hesitantly move to integrate, often taking precautions to keep the first attempts quiet and unpublicized.

When one of the first theaters in Memphis was attempting a low-key integration, I was asked along with Albert and two other African Americans to drive over from Jackson to do this, to protect local people from possible retaliation. We were to sit together in the main floor seats. We were warned to be ready for possible attack or arrests.

The theater managers and ushers had practiced the drill of trying to look nonchalant while rushing our little group in and seating us quickly. With eye-darting alertness, they anticipated problems.

As we watched *Lawrence of Arabia*, we were often paying more attention to any sounds around us in the auditorium than to the camels galloping out of the desert mirages on the screen.

8

Our local Jackson NAACP chapter met in a church sanctuary regularly to assess progress and formulate subsequent plans. We invited out-of-town guest speakers to offer us advice and encouragement. Medgar Evers came from his civil rights activities in Mississippi and met with our group.

Albert presented a report on the local demonstrations, and I related the progress of the interracial discussion groups. Then Medgar Evers spoke. He offered analysis of the activities nationally and urged sustained efforts locally until all goals toward equality were achieved.

After the meeting, Albert and I drove Medgar Evers back to Albert's home where he was staying overnight. The three of us went in and began to talk. He was going over episodes in his own efforts and projecting outcomes. We talked until after 2:00 a.m. He said calmly that he would probably be killed in Mississippi and that it probably could not be avoided. He said he would not leave the area to protect himself and that he would continue his activities. He added that there would be martyrs in the cause of civil rights but that martyrdoms should only encourage all of us to increase our activities, never to abandon them.

Later that same year, we heard the news that Medgar Evers was murdered in his driveway. That night, Albert and I sat in the same room where we had talked with him and reviewed all that he had shared with us. Well after midnight, Albert said that he felt the big transition in racial attitudes would not take place in our adult generation, but in our childrens', as they had increasing contact, as laws and customs changed.

He said, being an only child himself, that he had always wanted a brother. I had a brother to whom I was close, but who had said that I was crazy to teach where I was, and that working for civil rights was stupid. I longed to have a brother with whom to share these things.

So Albert said, "Tonight let's declare ourselves brothers, forming an extended family, with our children being cousins, and we and our wives being uncles and aunts to each other's children." In homage to Medgar Evers, we shook hands and created an inclusive family.

9

In our travels, there were moments of mirth. Segregationists had said that racial mixing would lead to mongrelization. One weekend Albert was driving the car from Memphis back to Jackson, with another rider in the passenger front seat. I road in the back seat with an African-American lady, and I chanced to be holding, wrapped in a blanket, a sleeping little puppy that the front seat passenger had newly acquired and was taking home.

We stopped for gas at one of those dimly-lighted small town stations with three rest rooms, marked "Men," "Women," and "Colored." The white attendant was visibly upset by the apparent interracial couple with their baby in a blanket in the back seat. After washing the front windshield, he kept washing the back side windows over and over again, peering through the glass, trying to see the child in the blanket. After we had filled and paid, I lifted the flap covering the dog's face so the attendant could see him. The attendant stood aghast, his worst fears realized, a mongrel! As we sped off, we could see him, mouth agape, having dropped his window-cleaning equipment.

= = =

As Albert was planning a drive the following month during spring break to see his parents in Mississippi, I received a letter from an African-American friend with whom I had been in school in Ohio, one of those who had refused to ever come south. He had gone more northerly instead and had become a minister. The church sent him to an area no one else would serve in, what he described as a "combat zone." He wanted me to come during my school's spring break to speak to his congregation and "to walk with me to see the things I see." Albert urged me to go and find out what that "walk with me" would include.

I went. He met me at the airport looking worn out, thinner, wearing his black garb and cleric collar, too wide now that he had lost weight. He wanted me to go with him through his daily rounds to visit and serve parishioners in their needs. He walked me through the rooms of housing projects, pointed out the drug dealers lounging in the debris-strewn hallways, stepped over naked babies crying in their own filth on the concrete walkways, knocked on doors with multiple locks and chains.

"Stay by me," he said, "and you should be safe." This from the person who had a local radio program emphasizing racial harmony, for which some of his *brothers* had seen fit to threaten his life. He described how twice he had been robbed, beaten, and rolled in the gutter on these rounds.

He comforted the sick who had no family nor health care. We stood with a pregnant 13-year-old staring comatose out the window. We spoke with the woman with no more tears left after her third son had been shot and killed, this one gunned down at her front door lying in a pool of blood at her feet.

He stayed in the remnants of the old parsonage connected to the church. Bars tried to protect the windows and doors that had not already been broken in and boarded over. The smell of decay and waste pervaded everything. He had no staff. The remaining parishioners—the aged, the unemployed, the homeless, the surviving youth—had little income for donations. Denominational headquarters had planned to close the church to cut their losses until he had implored them to let him try. They told him it was hopeless, that the church was dead and the ghetto was rotting. The idealist in him had replied that the souls were alive and needed help.

After I had spoken to his congregation earlier in the day, the two of us sat at midnight in the decaying parsonage with police sirens wailing on the city streets. He said, "I want to introduce the arts—music, painting, literature, drama—to feed their spirits. All I need are funds, space, support, and time." He smiled at the irony, through his chronic exhaustion.

Meanwhile, while I had been shown through the wastes of Chicago slums, Albert had headed for Mississippi. There was a filling station halfway where he usually stopped for gas. He did again, but this time needed to use a restroom. This station only had two—men and women. There was none for "colored."

He went into the men's room. A service station customer saw him entering the room and shouted to all the others nearby to come and teach him a lesson he would never forget. They broke open the door and dragged him out, kicking him and hitting him, shouting to lynch him, kill him.

He leaped up, ran for his car, jumped in, locked the doors, and sped out of the station and onto the road. He knew that the gas station attendant realized his life was in danger and that he had to flee.

A few days later, as he drove back north, he stopped at the station and paid the attendant, who expressed relief that he was all right and expressed his regret that the event had taken place at his station.

When Albert returned from Mississippi and I came back from Chicago, we discussed the events, reflecting on the basic need for changes of perspective everywhere, when people can respect the rights of each individual, as they would wish their rights respected. We concluded there was a lot more work to be done.

10

By 1966, the excellent job that Albert was doing as Business Manager of Lane College had been noted among the leadership of other colleges. He was contacted by the President of Philander Smith College, an African-American college in Little Rock, asking him to drive to Little Rock to discuss a position as Business Manager. That resulted in his being offered the job, and he accepted, and his wife, Fanye Porter, was offered a position as Dean of Women, both to begin the coming school year in September.

The next Saturday he drove from Jackson to Little Rock to begin reviewing the college files, bookkeeping records, and other aspects of the new position. I had flown to Chicago that week to a professional conference, rooming at the conference hotel downtown.

Albert discussed aspects of his new duties with the president, who said he had a desperate need to fill another position and wondered if Albert knew of anyone who would fit the qualifications. He said that with a number of things being newly integrated which had previously been separate, a major change had come in school accreditation. Previously there had been very different standards for black schools and white schools, the former being very lax and the latter being much more strict, and this year the accreditation had been joined into a single standard of the stricter nature, which Philander Smith had to go through for the first time.

First, he explained, the person currently in the position of the Dean of Instruction, the position responsible for handling the accreditation review, along with the whole academic program, did not have a Ph.D. degree, and the accreditation required that he have one. Also he needed someone who had some experience with the accreditation procedure.

It happened in ongoing discussions Albert and I had, that I mentioned several times that I saw needs at Lane College that could be improved for the students, but the measures could not come from teachers, but would have to be implemented by the administration. I added that it was tempting to consider going into administration in order to address some of those considerations. Coincidently, I had just served on the accreditation committee at Lane College.

With this in mind, he told the president that he did know someone with a Ph.D. and accrediting experience who might be interested in the position as Dean of Instruction. However, he explained, the person he had in mind was white. The president replied that he didn't care, so long as he could get the school through accreditation.

He asked Albert for my phone number. Albert explained that I was at a conference in Chicago. The president asked which hotel.

So it was that at 10:00 that night, while I was in my Chicago hotel room after a full day of conference sessions, my room phone rang. The voice on the other end introduced himself as the president of Philander Smith College, summarized his desperate need for a Dean with the degree and experience, told me I had been recommended, and said he wanted to talk with me further.

I said I would be glad to accompany Albert the next weekend when he went to Little Rock to continue his preparation for his new position. The president said, no, he could not wait that long. He said he knew that to fly back to Jackson from Chicago I would have to change planes in Memphis, that he would drive from Little Rock to Memphis and meet me at the airport between planes to talk. I gave him the arrival and departure times and flight numbers.

We met, he reviewed his needs, I answered his questions, and he offered me the job. When Albert met me at the Jackson airport, I said that a funny thing happened on the way back to Jackson. Thus it was that we both started driving on Saturdays to Little Rock to prepare for our new positions.

11

Philander Smith College operated apartments near the campus, and I secured one a block away. Albert rented one floor of a two story house two blocks from campus. Our campus offices were down the hall from each other in the central building.

There was a state organization of the college and university administrators who supervised the academic programs, the Deans of Instruction, the Provosts, and other titles. The African-American school officers were being invited for the first time. I wanted Philander Smith to be represented, so I went to the statewide meeting.

As we gathered in our conference center, the president of the organization, from one of the largest state schools, was making the rounds to those he did not recognize from previous meetings. He introduced himself to me, but when I introduced myself and the school I represented, he cursed and hurried away, refusing to speak to me again during the entire conference. If, during the breaks, I approached him, he again cursed and moved away. One of the other administrators whispered to me, on one of those occasions, that their leader "had some problems," as did a few others who shared his values.

= = =

Along with accessing the faculty needs in each department and starting searches to fill needed positions and meeting with each department to review their internal structures, I began to receive forms and directions from the accrediting association in preparation for their visit. There were reams of documents to be filled out, comparisons of that information to the pages of standards, and worksheets prepared for changes that had to be made before the review team arrived.

I met with student groups who would be interviewed by the accreditors, to include them in the process. Albert worked to reorganize the business office along more efficient and up-to-date record-keeping practices.

When the team came, some of them referred to the process as a logistical nightmare. Coordinating where they needed to be, who they needed to see, and the documents that needed to be reviewed were just a few of the hurdles before us. Some of our faculty noted that they never had to do all this before, and others replied it was the downside of integration.

When I received confirmation that we had passed the accreditation process, there was rejoicing.

12

I began to receive invitations from white discussion groups in town that asked me to come tell them "what black people thought" and "how they felt." Albert suggested that I go and find out what it was all about and maybe there could be some teachable moments.

I asked groups why they had invited me, instead of an African American, to discuss this with them. Their replies were that they didn't know any African Americans or how to approach them. I would explain that I could help them with that and could arrange for a co-worker to come talk with them at their next meeting. They would say yes, but ask how did they need to prepare? Just be yourselves was the simple answer.

I would bring Albert the next time, and he would move them toward a growing understanding. Many would reflect that this was the first time they had had this kind of interracial dialogue, any previous contact having been with yardmen and other workers. Some groups asked both of us to join their meetings, and we were able to gradually bring others to help the groups become more diverse. One person explained later that "life changed the night you both came; it was like a dividing-line of before and after."

Albert and I had been to one such gathering on a night when afterward, as we neared our neighborhood, the streets were cordoned off with police cars stopping all traffic. Something had occurred that made them fear some racial outbreak was about to occur, and they were trying to clear the area. As they talked to drivers ahead of us, they sent them in the direction of what would be considered the black neighborhood or in the other direction toward the white neighborhood.

Our car's passengers perplexed them. They told me to get out and go home to my neighborhood and then told Albert to go to his neighborhood. Every time I tried to explain that I lived in the area, they responded with increasing loudness, *you can't possibly live here, go to your own home.* When I explained that I worked at the college and lived in its housing, they threw up their hands in exasperation and shouted to *go ahead but get off the street,* and they opened the way and let us through. We later asked neighbors what was happening, but no one knew, only that the blockade had been set up around the area.

13

I had included in the communication classes I had taught that people tend to interpret what they see in front of them by the concepts they have in their thoughts, assumptions, and biases rather than what is actually there. I had used many examples, but I was about to experience a classic one.

I received in the mail an alumni directory from Ohio University which had not only alphabetical listings, but graduates' names organized by geographic areas so alumni could locate others in their vicinity. The listing included work addresses and phone numbers without indicating the name of the employer.

I answered my office phone to hear a cheery voice say that he was a graduate of Ohio University, had just received his directory, and found that he and I were the only ones currently listed in Little Rock. He said he wanted to come by, pick me up the next day at my office, and take me to meet his friends for lunch at a local hotel dining room. We made the arrangement for the following day.

At the appointed time, my secretary led him into my office. The man's face was contorted and ashen, and his hands trembled. After my secretary had left, I motioned toward a chair, but the man refused to sit. He said, "Under the circumstances, of course, I cannot be seen in public with you or go to lunch with you, or introduce you to my friends. I had the address but had no idea what this place was until I got here." He edged toward the door and would not respond to my questions, repeating that he could never be seen "with one of you people."

As he opened the door, he turned and said, "You know, you could almost pass for white," as he slammed the door and ran down the hall. And I had a classic example that he saw what he imagined and responded to what lurked in his mind's preconception.

I went to Albert's office to describe what had just happened. He suggested that I call him and explain, to give him something new to think about and see where that might lead.

When I reached him by phone that afternoon, he gasped in surprise to find his racial projection had been wrong. He regrouped his thoughts and made the proposal that we do have a noon meal with his friends, but on certain conditions. First, he could not pick me up, for he could never afford to be seen "at that place" again, so I would have to meet him and his friends at the restaurant. Second, we could not talk with his friends about my present position. If it came up, he would try to maneuver the subject to something else. We would meet the next day.

Albert's response to the update was that the man would never be the same, that he was now forced to think about things anew. I arrived at the restaurant, the man scanning my features for any sign of his first assumptions. The friends were genial and naturally turned the conversation again and again to jobs and where I was employed. The man worked like a bull fighter to deflect the bull from goring him, with the horns representing the taboo subject. He sweated through it, finally announcing that we all had to leave, and we scattered, me back to my mysteriously amorphous place of employment.

Albert listened to my summary of events. He said we would probably never know the specific changes taking place in the man, yet he now had to face the fact that someone who shared the Ohio educational experience was happily working in a situation that had been previously inconceivable to him.

= = =

The Great Society programs of President Lyndon Johnson include significant funds for programs to help historically black colleges. Since I was the Dean of Instruction, the packets of information to submit applications for grants ended up on my desk and grew deeper and deeper. I took a briefcase of them to the president's office and asked, "We have the opportunity to write grants to enrich many aspects of our programs, and we should take full advantage of them. Who is our grant writer?"

He leaned across his desk, pointed an index finger at me and replied, "You are."

One of the areas that came our way focused on exchanges of faculty and students between historically white schools and historically black schools. Grant proposals reached administrators in northern schools as well.

One day, the president urgently called me to his office. He explained that he had just received a phone call from the president of a northern college that wanted to explore a grant-funded exchange with our school. The two presidents had gingerly approached this new area of possibilities. They both agreed to head a delegation from each institution to meet at a neutral city half-way between our two locations, at a hotel where a conference room could be rented to explore the issues involved.

My college president was apprehensive. He desperately wanted this to work out. But he expressed serious concern about going himself or sending anyone else, as he put it, "of his race," afraid they might somehow say the wrong thing and jinx the effort. "You know how your people think and how to talk to them," he told me, "so I'm sending you by yourself." He flew me off alone to the half-way city where the meeting was to take place, leaving me to explain my solo appearance.

I registered at the hotel, went to my room, and then walked toward the conference room that had been reserved. I entered first and waited in the empty chamber for the delegation to arrive. A few minutes later, the door hesitantly opened. In came, not the expected delegation, but a solitary person, an African American. We looked at each other, and as it dawned on us what had happened, we both began to laugh.

His school had hired him as their very first minority administrator or faculty member. His president desperately wanted this affiliation, but was fearful that some of them would say the wrong thing and botch the efforts. "You know how to talk to your people" had been the words sending this other single negotiator on his way.

We said simultaneously, "Let's do it all." "Yes." "Everything possible under the grant." "Yes." So it was settled instantly, and we two "delegations" went chuckling away from the sterile conference room, to a restaurant, to share our experiences and start writing the details of the proposal.

14

Albert wanted to move from a rental apartment into his own home. By this time, housing was technically open to everyone, but in practice, people found ways to avoid the issue. I went with Albert as he followed up housing ads listed in the paper, many of which were in traditionally white neighborhoods. When he phoned ahead, the house was available; when we arrived and they saw him in person, suddenly the house "had just been sold."

After weeks of this, an urban renewal project was announced, opening up a new neighborhood. Streets had been put in, and lot perimeters identified on maps, with an opening day announced for people to come and bid on lots.

An African-American civil rights lawyer suspected that information he received was different from information being given out to white inquirers. So he proposed that I take the task of finding out. Sure enough, they gave me the time for the opening of the "land rush" that was considerably earlier than they told him, the assumption apparently being that all the lots would be taken by the white lot claimers, so none would be available when the African Americans showed up.

Armed with this information, the black families seeking lots were notified of the earlier time. Almost all of the early white lot selectors withdrew their intentions of getting a lot in the new neighborhood when they saw African Americans also claiming spaces.

Albert wanted a corner lot. I wanted a pie-shaped lot with a small front yard but a big back yard. When we compared notes after choosing, we laughed to find out that our two selections were across the street from each other.

We bought our lots, built our houses, as other new houses were also going up throughout the neighborhood. One day I drove out to see the progress on the inside of my house after the outside had been completed. I found that every pane of glass had been smashed.

Albert and his wife Fanye, along with their son, Albert II, and daughter, Portia, moved into their new house, and I and my wife Helena along with my son, Allan II, and daughter, Divina, were in our home across the street.

Some time afterward, a highway department official informed me I would have to move because the highway department was taking my land, needed for continuing freeway construction.

Most of the lots had been purchased by that time. But unsold space still existed just on the other side of Albert's house. I purchased it with what the highway department was paying me for my property. The house, itself, was mine to move or sell. The builder said I could not relocate my house to the new site because of the flatness of the former property and the slope of the new ground.

I advertised the house for sale to be moved, and buyers with farm property purchased it. As my children and I watched from our new home, our former house was lifted up and moved down the street. I remember my daughter, suddenly experiencing the sense of loss and exclaiming, "Daddy, they're taking our house!"

I secured the information about its new location and took my children out to see it. The children said it seemed strange to see our house sitting out in the middle of a farm field.

= = =

Whenever either Albert or I found the time to mow our own lawn, we simply continued on to the other's lawn as well. One Saturday I was mowing in front of Albert's house. By now, people in town referred to our area as an African-American neighborhood, or, because it now housed so many lawyers, doctors, business owners, teachers, and administrators, some townspeople referred to it as the "gilded ghetto," a term that disturbed some of our neighbors.

Even though there were no through streets in the neighborhood, some of the curious drove up to look at the area. As I was mowing the lawn in front of Albert's home, a white woman drove around the block several times, more slowly each time and looked increasingly angry. Finally she stopped her car. She rolled down her window and motioned me over. She asked me if this was my house, and I explained I lived next door. Then she shouted at me that my soul was going to be damned for eternity for going against the teachings of Jesus Christ by living with "those people." She proclaimed that God, in the Bible, specifically ordered separation. Even worse, I was "helping one of them," while God forbade it.

I told her that I was unfamiliar with any such passages in the Bible and would appreciate her showing me the locations. She grabbed her Bible from the seat next to her, started thumbing through it, all the while never stopping the repetition of damnation for those who "mix," going against the direct commands of God. I asked her about references such as *even as ye do unto the least of these, my brethren, do you also unto me.* That only applied to human beings, not to them, she shouted. Her search and our exchange continued for well over an hour, until she threw the Bible into the passenger seat, jerked the car into gear, and screeched the tires taking off down the street.

= = =

At my UALR office, I received a request from the agency that had been involved in the development of my neighborhood, requesting my professional services as a communication specialist. As their housing projects were facing increasing integration, they wanted workshops with the tenants in the new developments. They also wanted communication workshops for their staff to help improve their interaction and effectiveness.

I conducted extensive interviews with people in their projects about their concerns and questions, and then created workshops to address these issues, and created and conducted personnel workshops. I worked with the agency for months on a variety of topics and enterprises.

One day I was in their office arranging for the next series of events when one of them asked me, for the first time, where I lived. When I told them, the whole room became hushed. One of them said, "Oh my God, he's the one!" What I then learned was that some of their personnel had deep problems with "that white person" who chose to move into what had become identified as a black neighborhood, and had even helped the black buyers to secure their lots.

There was a sudden dual reaction in two opposite directions. On the one hand, we had experienced months of positive relations together in my capacity as a communications consultant. On the other hand, they suddenly identified me as "that person" for whom they had no charitable feelings.

Some staff found it difficult to even communicate with me. After several weeks, I found they had sought other professionals to carry on the consulting work but found no one. They realized that the UALR faculty was dedicated to the "urban mission" of the university, which was to offer our services to the community at reduced rates. Ours were far below what would normally be charged, and they realized they could save their own resources by continuing to work with me. However, some of their former friendliness was gone.

Albert and I discussed this, and he expressed his confidence that the individuals were facing some new realities of their own and doing some soul-searching. This would be an ongoing teachable change as their previously unchallenged personal prejudices had something new to face and adjust to. Sure enough, as time passed, their interactions with me reframed into more positive ones.

15

Albert wanted to offer his children the option of selecting any university in the country that they wished to attend and be able to finance their schooling. He knew that his salary at the college would not be sufficient for that.

As social change took place, companies that had not previously had interracial staff began to seek out qualified African Americans for their first attempts to integrate. When Albert was offered the position as the "first" in a company, at a salary substantially above the one at the college, he decided to change jobs.

As I met coworkers from his new employment, they said his presence in their office had made a positive influence on the whole staff. They complimented his professional competence as an accountant and his ease in interacting with them as an individual. Some told me that he was the first "minority" person they had ever known as an individual, and that interaction with him had changed their stereotyped preconceptions.

= = =

As I continued to write grants for the college for new and innovative programs, resources grew rapidly. The grants for exchange programs between historically black and historically white schools brought white exchange students from colleges in the north-central and northeast states. Our students from Philander Smith, in turn, went to take classes there for a year.

Faculty exchanges with the same schools brought white faculty to Philander Smith as our counterparts taught in their schools. The participants in both directions reported that they were able to learn from their new associates and share ideas with them as well.

One of the white exchange students appeared in my college office one day, closed the door and leaned against the wall breathing rapidly. She explained she was having a "nerves attack" as she realized for the first time what it was like being "a minority." The students had interacted with her in classes, but no one had included her in any outside activities, even though she was living in a campus dormitory.

She said that for the first time she felt what all of the "first Negroes" to integrate the various schools were experiencing. She talked at length until her breathing normalized and she seized upon a resolution to address her tensions. She vowed to make extensive notes about all the feelings she was having and what kind of actions on the part of others could alleviate her feelings of emptiness, separation, loneliness, and despair. Then when she would return to her school up north, she would identify each new "minority student" coming to the school, and offer friendship, concern, and interaction to help them.

She kept her notes and acted on her growing insights, and we continued to communicate after she returned to her school. She reported on the successes she was experiencing in "living her plan." She found that in every program in which she participated, on or off campus, she would search for "minority individuals" and instantly approach them to help bring them into the activities.

= = =

So many of our students had attended under-equipped and under-staffed elementary and high schools, that many lacked fully-developed skills for college-level classes. I wrote major grants for materials and personnel to help remedy this, and resources poured in. Students going to the new skills development center were making up for years of deprivation, and this helped change the whole outcome of their college experiences.

Grants were funded to support cooperative programs among historically Black colleges to see how they could reinforce their common goals and activities. I flew off to meetings with administrators from those schools, being, myself, the minority in the group.

= = =

The director at the Methodist Student Center at Little Rock University (LRU) was concerned that their students, all white, needed an opportunity to interact with African-American students. He phoned me and arranged for me to

57

bring a group of students from Philander Smith College (PSC) to meet a group of LRU students.

I drove with our students to the center, and the director said to the combined group that this was, to his knowledge, the first time there had ever been an interracial student group meeting on campus. Individuals introduced themselves, and then the director invited the students from both schools to ask students from the other campus about anything they wanted to know. The interaction lasted all afternoon.

In 1969, Little Rock University joined the University of Arkansas System and became the University of Arkansas at Little Rock (UALR). Along with this change, integration took place, and students at PSC realized that the tuition at the state school was lower than at their private school.

Some PSC students enrolled in UALR, but found little social involvement. Accordingly, after their classes they returned to the PSC campus to socialize with their friends.

Groups of those students would come to my office and tell me the stories of the problems some of the UALR faculty and students had with their presence on campus. One student described how one of her teachers, when asking for student responses from her class, would ignore her raised hand as if she did not exist. Others described their attempts to become involved in various student organizations only to be rejected.

One day the group that came to my office had a request. Please, they said, get a job at UALR so we will have a refuge on campus where we can go to discuss our problems and have a place where we can relax. They said that I had accomplished good things at PSC, but now they needed me to help them at the other campus.

= = =

Shortly thereafter, the PSC president called me to his office. He said the board had told him to tell me to stop all the grant writing and not to start any new programs for 10 years, and then they would decide if they would permit any changes after that decade had passed.

I explained to the president that I could not in good conscience ignore grant opportunities for advancement of our students and staff, and therefore if this restriction was going to be enforced, I would leave my position at the end of the school year.

16

As I faced unemployment, my phone rang. The caller introduced himself as the founder and director of Arkansas Enterprises for the Blind. He had heard of my "fine and innovative work" at the college, and because of it, he wanted to offer me a job.

Arkansas Enterprises for the Blind, as the first training center for the adult visually impaired in the world, had continuing requests from state agencies across the United States and from newly developing agencies in other countries to come to Little Rock to learn the training skills. He explained that he needed a coordinator of the program with educational experience who had a Ph.D. to give the program "creditability."

I accepted the position. As Director of Research and Staff Development, I was also responsible for writing grants for training the visually impaired in new job opportunities, such as being information specialists for the IRS for people calling in with questions.

I found myself flying to Washington to meet with officials to work out details for new grants. In the meantime, I was organizing the individualized programs for the people from other states and countries to provide them with the training that would enable them to return to their home areas and establish services there.

After the program had been fully organized and functioning, there was one big step the director still wanted to take. He wanted to offer academic credit and a degree to these professional trainees. I pointed out that right across the street from Enterprises for the Blind was the University of Arkansas at Little Rock. I had met its chancellor and found him to be as creative and determined as the director was.

I suggested I get the two of them together over lunch, and I predicted that by the end of lunch, they would have worked out an agreement whereby the university could offer a rehabilitation training degree program with the training to take place at the Enterprises for the Blind.

The lunch occurred, and agreement was reached by the time dessert was finished, and the cooperative program got underway. With that in place, I felt ready to return to teaching.

On a lunch hour, I walked from my Enterprises office across the street to the UALR campus and looked up an administrator who had been so dedicated to integration that he had previously offered his services as a part-time teacher at Philander Smith, where we found we had a lot in common in our concepts of human unity.

At his university office, I explained my situation. He took me to the Provost's office, who in turn took me to the office of the chair of the communication department. The chairperson said they had no positions, but questioned me on my background and specialties. He said he did not have any more time right at the moment, but asked that I drop back tomorrow again at lunch time.

I did return, and he said a position had suddenly become available overnight and offered it to me. I said yes and joined the faculty at UALR.

That same day, the Provost called me back in and explained that while the student body was integrating, the faculty and administration had not. He said he wanted to move in that direction immediately and had a position open for the Director of Testing. He added that he did not want to "steal" any personnel from PSC, but since I had been there, he asked if I had anyone I could recommend for the position.

When he described the qualifications, I immediately thought of Albert's wife, Fanye Porter. I phoned her, and when she expressed interest, I went and picked her up, drove her to campus, and took her to the Provost's office where he described in detail the position and salary. She accepted. He said she would need an assistant in the position and they could discuss that later. When they did, she recommended an outstanding student from PSC, and he was hired, rising eventually to become a vice-chancellor.

Having filled these two positions, the Provost told me he was very happy that we had taken the first steps to integrate the university personnel, opening the way for more to follow.

With Fanye and me now working at UALR, and my wife, Helena, working at a location along the route to Albert's workplace, every morning I would pick up Fanye and drive to work, while Albert picked up Helena, and they drove to work, reversing the directions for the return home each evening.

I kept connections with Philander Smith and Arkansas Enterprises for the Blind. In advanced communication classes at UALR where each student performed communication assistance to an outside organization, benefiting that organization and providing the student with practical experience, I was able to arrange for UALR students to have intern experiences at PSC.

When AEB wanted to offer college preparatory classes for students hoping to go to college, I taught those classes at AEB to help prepare them for their coming experiences.

17

Gradually, each time my children were with their grandparents on our visits to Albuquerque, my parents grew accustomed to hearing about Uncle Albert, Aunt Fanye, cousin Portia, and cousin Albert II. My parents finally came to Little Rock to visit.

By this time, my children would talk about how our family had two houses. To use them both, they had decided they would sleep over at "our other house" every Friday night, and it became a weekly event. Their eagerness to show my parents "the other house" took the form of their grabbing their grandparents' hands and leading them over next door, an invitation which my parents could not refuse.

In this way, they met Albert and his family. I could see a change in my parents on a daily basis. For the first time in their lives, they were getting to know as individual people with personalities, interests, and experiences, what had always been a category. The conversations grew. Connections strengthened. They saw the Porters helpfulness and kindness, and observed the love their grandchildren had for their uncle, aunt, and cousins.

And then, like the sun coming out from behind prolonged dark clouds, my mother said to me and the children, "You know, every family needs an Uncle Albert." I remembered her saying previously, on hearing that I was going to an African-American school to teach, that it would have been better if I had never been born, and now we exited from that with a new understanding and relationship.

From then on in our phone conversations, she would always ask about Fanye, Albert, Portia, and Albert II. And if, for some reason, she needed to call me and could not reach me, she would call Albert to check up on me and to deliver messages.

= = =

The International Visitors Program funded by the State Department brought to America politicians and business people from other countries to experience first-hand a variety of American cities and people. The national office arranged for visits to cities, hosted by local Councils of International Visitors. The guests would be scheduled during the day to meet with officials and professionals related to their positions in their own countries. One feature the visitors requested was a home visitation for a meal with an American family to get the feeling of a U.S. household.

Albert had been concerned that those visitations included only white households, not giving the visitors the wider exposure to the American population. He volunteered his efforts to find African-American hosts as well. Both he and I were asked to serve on the Board of the Arkansas Council of International Visitors.

He and I volunteered to host the visitors, with both of our families joining together for the evening meal, where the guests would hear our children refer to their aunts and uncles and cousins. Visitors often expressed their surprise at this unanticipated family, saying it was not what they expected after studying U.S. history.

= = =

Albert and I were still receiving invitations from groups in other cities to come and help facilitate interracial discussion groups. We also received invitations to fly to Canada to explain to groups in several cities what was "really going on in the southern U.S.A."

In one city, which had been one of the end points of the underground railroad in the 1800s, there were many descendants of the escaped slaves. A group of these African Canadians came to one meeting. As the white chairperson of the evening was introducing us, she noted that while they were interested in learning from the two speakers about the events in the southern U.S., no such problems existed in their area and country, and everyone was considered equal in all ways.

As she spoke, I noticed that the African Canadians were exchanging glances and facial expressions that subtly but clearly suggested disagreement. As soon as our discussion with the audience ended, one of the African Canadians hurried over and said they all wanted to meet with us in her home afterward to tell us more.

At her home, we talked for hours, as they explained that while there were no segregation laws as there had been in the United States, there were still individuals who had a long way to go to consider people equal, and that they ran into individual discrimination on a daily basis.

18

Albert and I considered that helping with other areas of community service were extensions of our civil rights work. We received invitations to serve on various boards and commissions. We both served on the boards of Treatment Homes working with foster children, the Arkansas Supportive Housing Network working with the homeless, Volunteers in Public Schools, Weekend Theater, Arkansas Friends of the Zoo, the Japan-American Society.

To raise funds to buy Christmas presents for all of the foster children of Treatment Homes, Inc. (THinc), there evolved the holiday sales of gingerbread houses. At first THinc both baked and then assembled them, but as demand grew, the pre-baked parts were purchased commercially which then needed to be assembled. Albert volunteered to do that, and he would put together one thousand houses each year. Using icing to secure the structures together, the walls had to dry before the roof could be added, so there were lines of partially assembled houses lining several rooms of his house for weeks. Each morning we would load a car with the finished gingerbread houses and drive them to the Treatment Homes offices downtown, and then pick up more parts to assemble that day.

The fragrance of gingerbread so permeated his home and seeped outside, that it could be detected a half block away. He deservedly became nicknamed "the Gingerbread Man." Not one to waste any resource, when some of the pieces of walls or roofs had been cracked or broken when being shipped to Treatment Homes, Albert took those and patched the pieces together with the icing, not to sell but to give to other children as holiday gifts.

Then at the annual holiday party, with the staff, foster parents, and foster children together, Santa would appear, taking each child in turn, and presenting a present that the money from the gingerbread houses had purchased.

= = =

We were invited to a conference that took us to France. Conference side trips included the rounds of Paris landmarks. Standing and looking at the Eiffel Tower, Albert recalled his days in the military in France and the tragic circumstances of war-torn Europe.

Conference travel took us on to the Palace of Versailles. As we toured its grand halls with the guide, we heard how it had become the center of political power in France when Louis XIV moved there from Paris in 1682. It remained so until the outbreak of the French Revolution when, in 1789, the royal family returned to Paris.

In the Galerie des Glaces, the Hall of Mirrors, we heard of the many ceremonies held there and how it had become a symbol of great wealth as contrasted to the poverty outside. Even there, as Albert and I stood in the multiple reflections, people approached us with questions about segregation and discrimination in the United States, and how our working together had come about.

= = =

With the organization that secured housing for the homeless in central Arkansas, there were periods of time between the negotiations for the house and its occupancy. During that period, the lawns of those houses needed to be mowed, raked, and trash cleaned up. On many of our Saturdays, Albert and I would load a lawnmower, rakes, and trashbags into the trunk of the car and head out to take care of the houses until they were occupied.

We both served on the Task Force to develop the Racial and Cultural Diversity Commission for the city of Little Rock. When the long work of developing that was completed, we both were asked to serve on the newly formed Commission.

In addition, Albert served on the Leadership Roundtable Association, Arkansas Lighthouse for the Blind, the Governor's Advisory Committee on Aging, the Arkansas Fairness Council, the Centers for Youth and Families, New Futures for Little Rock Youth, Little Rock Sister Cities Commission, Southwestern Bell Senior Advisory Panel, National Committee to preserve Social Security and Medicare. I was serving on the board of Friends of the Arts, Oasis Renewal Center, Community Concerts, The Agency on Aging, Shepherd Center, Pulaski

County Historical Society, Adventures in Learning Committee of LifeQuest of Arkansas and its Task Force for the Third Age Initiative, and as president of the Bookfellows Society. We found all these to be extensions of our overall goal to help serve community needs, and to encourage these groups to be as diverse as possible.

19

Valuing family connection, Albert decided his extensive family on his mother's side needed to stay in contact. His mother was one of 13 children who had married and had children of their own and grandchildren, had moved all over the country, and never had occasion to all come together and were losing touch. So he decided to organize a family reunion. It was no simple task. It meant gathering addresses, contacting people, getting feedback on how many would be coming, securing space for them to stay and meet, arranging meals and setting up sessions for them to introduce themselves, hold discussions, and socialize as a family.

We filled pages with addresses, calling some to get addresses and phone numbers of others, mailed out information, contacted hotels to secure price lists, and gradually the event took shape.

Albert envisioned having a reunion every two years, letting family members volunteer to host it in different locations each time. He would hold the first one in Little Rock as a prototype. When the gathering took place, the attendees received a packet with a program of events, the names of everyone attending, and a tee-shirt proclaiming, "Jackson Family Reunion."

Getting the tee-shirts made was a challenge, having to secure by phone and mail the needed sizes, which ranged from small to XXX large.

The "official" photo of everyone gathered together in his front yard included my two children in the center of the front row with this, their extended family. Large-size copies of the picture were mailed out across the country to all of the participants afterward.

Before some of my family reunions, several of my family who had met Albert would communicate with me to be sure to bring him. After one of my relatives met him for the first time at such an event, and they had talked at length, my relative exclaimed, "My gosh! He's an educated person!"

= = =

Albert's mother was injured in a car accident in Mississippi. When she was released from the hospital, she was bedridden, and her husband could not lift nor move her to provide the care she needed. Albert brought her to Little Rock, wanting her to be with family rather than in a nursing home. He lifted her out of bed to seat her in a chair and back again, cooked and served her meals, and came home from his job every noon to tend to her.

By this time, trips to Albuquerque to see my parents had become regular events several times a year. The car did not provide space for my children to stretch out and sleep during the long drive, so when friends were getting rid of an old van, I bought it, and the Albuquerque journey became more comfortable.

The van also proved to be helpful for transporting Albert's mother. Sitting in a car was almost impossible for her, and Albert wanted to drive her back to her home in McComb, Mississippi, frequently where she could keep up with her friends. The van had seats that folded out into beds, and this worked perfectly for the trips.

Getting her from bed into the van in a wheelchair from an upstairs bedroom proved challenging. We experimented with the process until we found the method that worked.

It seemed to breathe new energy into her to go back to her home, so Albert decided to hold the next family reunion in McComb. We began the process of letters, phone calls, room reservations, food arrangements, working several months in advance to complete the process. Then two days before the reunion, Albert and I, with his mother loaded in the van, along with our wives and children, headed for Mississippi, along with piles of tee shirts. This time the shirts were imprinted with a map of the United States showing the locations of all family members.

= = =

When Albert's father's health deteriorated to the point where he needed daily care, Albert brought him to Little Rock. Albert was cooking for them, feeding them, bathing them, washing their bedding and their clothes, all this in addition to his work schedule.

When both Albert and Fanye had to be out at meetings in the evenings, I would stay with his parents. His father's condition worsened, with increasing labored breath. They had just come into the house downstairs one evening when his father's breathing produced a long wheezing. The term I had heard, "death rattle," came to mind, and this was, in fact, his father's final breath. His pulse was gone, and I rushed downstairs to get them. That had been his final moment.

= = =

Albert's mother, now an invalid and a widow, found comfort in the memories of what had been, which were symbolized by her home in McComb. Albert wanted to keep up their home so he could take her back for visits to provide her that degree of comfort. But there was no one there to take care of the house and yard.

So once a month he and I would drive down to McComb, leaving by 4:00 a.m. on a Saturday morning, to mow and rake the yard, inspect the house, and check for any repairs needed. He had the utility bills mailed to his Little Rock address.

Then every few weeks we took his mother in the van to her home in McComb, phoning ahead to let her friends know she was returning so they could come and spend time with her while Albert and I worked on the yard and repairs.

= = =

When some of our organizations had national conferences in various cities, as we drove there and back, we would stop along the way to see his relatives and mine. The effect continued to be interesting to observe. For some of our family members, this was their first extended exposure to interracial communication with an individual.

= = =

I was approached about starting a scout troop in my area of town. The person mentioning it said I would not have to worry about anyone causing trouble by trying to integrate it, since the groups were kept separate. I explained that I would not consider it unless it was integrated, that those interested deserved to have the experience in a diverse group as part of their learning experience.

So the boys from the surrounding area were invited and appeared at my home for the weekly meetings in a nicely diverse group. We went on camping trips. On one of those occasions at a scout camp after dark, the camp coordinator guided us by flashlight to the place to pitch our tents. We did, got into them, and the rain started. Those of us in my tent suddenly realized that there was a stream of water flowing under one side of the tent and out the other. The coordinator had placed us on a hillside atop a little run-off gully, being no problem when dry, but flowing when it rained. When we all rolled our sleeping bags to the edges of the tent, the water flowed through the center of the tent the rest of the night, not dampening us at all.

= = =

One of my university students who had come from China arrived to my office one day looking panicked. Here she lived with a host family that she felt comfortable with at first. Now something had changed when they started sharing their ideas.

She explained that her host family had seemed to be sensible, rational people at first. Now, she said, she feared for their sanity and therefore for her own safety. They were telling her that strength comes from the length of one's hair. They believed that snakes talked. They believed that there were non-humans that looked like humans but had big wings. They believed that dead people had been brought back to life. They believed that women could be created out of a rib-bone from a man. They thought that people could walk on top of water even when it was not frozen into ice. Now they wanted to take her to a place to meet other people with the same misconceptions, and she was afraid to go there.

She felt that if they had these delusions they might be going crazy and even try to harm her. She wondered if she should move elsewhere or maybe even leave school and go back to China. She had never been exposed to any religious organizations at home in an atheistic environment, and this encounter with the stories of Samson, the Garden of Eden, and angels had produced a major culture shock.

We began a series of discussions that amounted to a short course on the history of the Bible. She concluded that it had a lot of "mythology and miracles" mixed with "suggestions for living a good life." She also concluded that the material in the first category was irrelevant, while the behavioral admonitions were relevant. Her anxiety decreased, and she remained with her host family, hoping she could help them become more scientific in their thinking and less superstitious.

20

With both of us members of the board of the Arkansas Council of International Visitors and my teaching the Intercultural Communication courses at the university, Albert and I were members of the World Communication Association. The international professional organization met each time in a different country where the members could gather useful materials and then travel together to adjoining countries to develop additional insights.

We spoke at conference sessions about interracial communication and human rights and received invitations to other international conferences to speak. We journeyed to Egypt to address the Association for the Advancement of Policy Research and Development in the Third World, which included a boat trip up the Nile with stops at historic sites. We rode camels around the pyramids, strode about the columns of the temples of Luxor and Karnak, as Egyptian anthropologists described their history going back to the 27th century B.C.

In Egypt, the first time some children came up to us and asked Albert if they could rub his head, we asked for an explanation. They said, from his looks, he was certainly Nubian, and everyone knew that it was good luck to rub a Nubian's head. In various locations, other people approached with the same request. On finding out where we were from, some assured him that although he was from Arkansas, he was still Nubian, and they still wanted the head rub. He genially bent over so they could secure their good luck. Adults, hearing of our home area, asked about the terrible things they heard about the southern United States and how the two of us had come to know each other under such conditions.

This same curiosity persisted in England at the conference we addressed at Cambridge University. A participant, knowing we had to return to London for our flight asked if he could drive us there so he could ask questions about our human rights experiences.

He recommended we take advantage of the time in London, suggesting that we line up at the theatre where the *Phantom of the Opera* was playing, for the few extra tickets they sometimes had just before the usually sold-out performances. Again, as we conversed with other people in line, they had extensive questions about our experiences. Eventually, we secured two seats, sat in the center orchestra section, listened to the phantom sing, and watched the chandelier fall on cue.

After a conference in Finland, the participants took a boat to St. Petersburg, Russia, and an overnight train to Moscow. In Red Square and the Kremlin, we were approached by people, and one of them who spoke English would translate their questions and our responses about what the real conditions were like in America and how was it possible for us to know each other.

In Budapest, Hungry, still under Communist rule, in our conference hotel room we discovered first one hidden microphone embedded in the wooden panel of the desk, and then another, and a dozen more, hidden in shelving, bureaus, and pictures. Other participants found the same in each of their rooms so all conversations in the rooms could be monitored.

Conference participants were warned not to ride the buses around Budapest, as citizens were not to mingle with outsiders. Albert and I decided to do so anyway as the only realistic way to get around to see both Buda and Pest on opposite sides of the Danube river. Although people might look around them before speaking to us, their curiosity overcame them, and they, too, had questions.

In China, on an information-gathering project for sabbatical study related to intercultural communication classes, in the off-season with many guides, translators, and drivers idle until the tourist season, we were offered inexpensively the services of a driver and translator/guide. In one city, they were dropping us off at the huge hotel, saying they would pick us up the next morning. We asked where exactly to meet them in the mammoth block-long lobby. The guide said that everyone there would know exactly where we were at all times, and they could ask anyone.

When they picked us up, our next stop was the Great Wall of China. It was the time of the Chinese New Year, when the tourists were primarily from other localities in China, not from other countries. Albert and I were a distinct novelty and had conversations on the Great Wall answering questions about human rights in America.

In Tokyo, Japan, there is an orange replica of the Eiffel Tower. In the room at the top of the tower with a 360 degree view of the city, we heard from a group of school-age children murmurs of "Americans, English, practice." Suddenly we were surrounded by a class of children, all studying English, instructed to take every opportunity to practice. The first student spoke very precisely, "Are you American? Do you speak English? May we speak with you? May we practice our English? Thank you." And they proceeded with a series of rehearsed questions: What is your occupation? Do you have children? How many of them? How old are they? Do you enjoy our country? Many questions were repeated several times by different students for practice. We inquired as to whether we could ask them questions, and they helped each other build responses.

21

In India, when we arrived at Agra, we heard the stories of the Taj Mahal, walked along its reflecting pools, and heard the historian describe its background. When Shah Jahan, titled the King of the World, crowned himself in 1628, his constant companion was his wife Mumtaz Mahal. When she died, he built this glistening white marble monument to her. There were plans for a duplicate in black stone, which was never completed, but its foundation still remains.

We learned at the Observatory in Jaipur of its construction in 1727 by Maharaja Sawai Jai Singh, who had ascended the throne at the age of 11. The several large instruments are as much architectural works as scientific instruments dealing with astronomical phenomena. Early on, word of it spread, attracting people as far away as Europe to come and study there.

Khajuraho was the site where, between the ninth and 12th centuries, more than 80 temples existed, adorned with exquisite layers and levels of statuary. The more than 20 temples that survive are now preserved for their historic and artistic significance. From the archeologists' explanations, the structures may be thought of as three-dimensional stories of history, legends, and mythology.

In Delhi, the National Capital Territory of India, including New Delhi, the territorial capital, we were told it would be "crowded," understandably with its 22 million people. We walked the streets where the old and new mixed in a panorama of centuries.

Before going to India, we heard from a previous traveler there that he had seen on the densely crowded streets the body of a person who had died and the body remained unmoved for a time, with people simply stepping around or over it. That foreshadowing came to mind when we experienced it.

Others had told us not to be surprised if we were frequently approached by people begging for money. Of the times we encountered that, the most persistent was a man who followed alongside us for two miles, never ceasing his well-practiced entreaties, until we reached our hotel and the doorman pointed at him and then at the street.

= = =

When apartheid was being challenged in South Africa, our communication conference was invited to hold its meeting there with the understanding that the diversity of our organization would be welcomed without restriction.

When the conference organizers asked that the participants be permitted to see the black as well as the white sections of the city, the officials agreed. When they guided us to the parking area to start the tour, we found our transportation consisted of heavily armored military vehicles with bulletproof glass. Even though we were driven through these areas within the city, we had been denied the opportunity to travel outside the city to the black townships to see conditions there.

Another request of the conference had been to have some speakers from the black townships come to speak to the group. One of those became very curious about Albert and me. He took Albert aside and asked if he would like to visit his home in the township. Albert said yes, but only if I could come too. The man said we could do it that night under the cover of darkness, that I would have to hide in the back of the car, for I could not be seen entering the township.

We proceeded, ending up at his home, shielding me as he hurried me inside. We talked with his family, who had as many questions for us as we did for them. Later in the evening, his father reached over and took my hands and with tears in his eyes said this was the first time in his life that one "of my background" had ever entered his house and talked with him.

The man returned us unobtrusively to our hotel, glad that no "incident" had occurred. But the next day, the local conference planner took me aside and said he had heard what we had done, going to the township the night before. "Don't you know," he said, "that by doing that you could have caused an international incident? That is simply not permitted."

Many of the local white participants talked about the numbers of white South Africans who were considering leaving the country, fearing that if apartheid ended, there would be a blood-bath slaughtering the white population.

Back in Little Rock, we followed the news daily of the changing conditions in South Africa. And then came an unexpected contact from South Africa. Some officials felt that Albert and I had found a peaceful, comfortable, respectful cooperation, and could help them understand what they could do to help have such a transition in their country. They asked if they could send a delegation to Little Rock to talk with us at length to share our insights that could assist them in the circumstances they faced. Their delegation came, and we talked and shared and answered questions, grateful that we could be of service.

= = =

We attended a conference in Brazil, speaking at sessions in Rio de Janeiro. There was a former student from Rio who had enrolled in my university graduate classes in Little Rock. Before her return to Brazil, she had invited us to contact her if we ever came to Rio.

When such a communications conference did occur in Rio, at the opening session the participants received a presentation from the local coordinators on the do's and don't's of navigating in the city. One admonition was to never ride the buses, that pickpockets were rampant and foreigners were a favorite target.

When I contacted my former student and told her this when we got together, she said, "Nonsense. You've got to experience riding the buses around town. Just don't keep your wallet in the usual back pocket, put it in your shirt pocket and button your coat, and, anyway, I can spot the pickpockets." She added that she would show us places we would not otherwise see, and we proceeded on our personalized tour. Another admonition of hers was not to ride in a car with anyone after dark who actually stopped at stoplights, because thieves waited at traffic lights to smash car windows of those who stopped and then rob them.

She guided us to the "must-sees" of the top of Corcovado Mountain, crowned by the 1,200-ton, 130-foot statue of Christ the Redeemer and on to the cable car ride to the top of Pao de Acucar, the often-pictured Sugarloaf Mountain, for a meal at the summit restaurant.

During the conference, we heard discussions about how, behind the façade of apparent mixing and equality among the Brazilians of Indian, European, and African ancestry, there were significant racial divides, and we were taken to some of the slum areas to illustrate the point. Once again, we found ourselves the object of curiosity and questions about the racial divides in the United States.

The conference organizers arranged for journeys by boat up the Amazon River into the jungles. An anthropologist led us into the jungle villages of native tribes. As I took notes for future classes, I asked, as we approached one village, the nature of some of the legends and mythologies. These people have none, the anthropologist said, explaining that they were coastal dwellers and all of their ancestral stories had related to the ocean and water. When the Portuguese came, the tribe escaped into the jungle far from the ocean to avoid being enslaved. The new generations born away from the water had no reference to understand the old stories, and the legends had ceased to be repeated. We spent much of the day with the tribal members, in the middle of the village, discussing the events that now made up their lives.

22

A focus of constant discussion wherever Albert and I traveled related to the inner qualities of the people we met, whatever their outer appearance. We shared these observations at some of our presentations on intercultural communication.

Following one of the presentations we were asked to lead a weekend children's activities group in this process of identifying inner qualities rather than exterior appearances.

Starting the first class, I requested the children to name as many negative qualities as they could. They shouted out dozens of them. Asked to act them out, one by one, they could.

When asked to name all the positive qualities they could, they were nearly silent, only coming forth with "good." When requested to act out that quality, they all sat silently doing nothing.

Adults are often quick to identify negative behavior in children, calling it by name, so the child has a word and an example of action to define that term. Less often, adults commend positive behavior, naming it and calling attention to the actions it refers to.

So we started our list: truthfulness, trust, honesty, kindness, and with each term talked about how to act it out. Thereafter, we encouraged the children to call attention to examples of behavior that demonstrated each of the traits we had discussed.

As the classes continued, the list grew, and their ability to attach words to the actions around them brought forth a new kind of bonding and development. Every positive attribute they could identify in others, they could also look for in themselves, and behaviors began to change to more and more positive interaction. They found they could feel good about themselves without being self-centered but being virtue-centered, honoring these qualities.

We asked them to describe each other in terms of these positive qualities rather by physical attributes. So instead of tall, short, fat, thin, blond, brunette came humorous, helpful, considerate, and happy. The list continued to grow: courteous, sincere, industrious, calm, focused, careful, thoughtful, dependable.

The children began to identify others as a unique combination of qualities without resorting to gender, race, size, or ethnicity. We had them try describing their family members this way, and a new appreciation of their family members developed.

Other groups heard of these sessions and asked for similar classes for their children. My son was in one of these groups, and we had already been exploring these same perspectives at home. Then a phone call came one evening from his fourth-grade teacher. She quickly told me not to be alarmed by a call from a teacher, which usually meant a problem; in this case, she hastened to explain, this was just the opposite.

She described how in her class during recreational periods, the children tended always to group by gender and race, dividing up as "white girls, black girls, white boys, black boys, Hispanic boys...etc." There was only one child, she said, who went to all the groups and seemed not only unaware of the differences, but also to see wonderful qualities in all of the individuals. "And your son even describes the most wonderful qualities that he sees in me," she said, "just astounding me and making me more conscious of applying them. And he has done more to bring together the class by going from group to group and bringing diverse people together. Once he mentions good qualities in others, they start to repeat them."

Finally she asked, "What I'm calling you about, what I want to know is, how did this happen? What can explain this? I really want to know."

I shared how Albert and I had worked for so long to help people see beyond race, ethnicity, gender, and all other designations that divide people into categories, to see individuals as unique combinations of virtues that cross all categorical barriers. I described how the application of becoming conscious of positive qualities in one's self and others can change families and all groups, helping to change society one virtue-sighting at a time. She said that she could already anticipate how this would influence her group activities in the future.

23

Our combined families' interactions during the times of civil rights transitions lent itself to daily possibilities of interesting circumstances.

In third grade when my son brought home a friend one afternoon, he introduced us where I was working in the yard, and then we saw Albert walking over from next door. "And this is my Uncle Albert," my son said. The friend looked in surprise and said, "He can't be your uncle. He's..." But before he could finish, my son put his hand on his friend's arm and said, "Accept it, just accept it."

= = =

One year when Albert's daughter, Portia, returned home from Oberlin College for Christmas break, she brought a friend, who happened to be white. UALR was still in session, and Portia asked if they could come and sit in on one of my communication classes.

As we entered the classroom, I said to the class, "I want to introduce you to my niece and her friend from Oberlin." Immediately one of my outspoken students said, "Well, I guess we know which one is your niece." To which Portia responded, putting her hand on my shoulder, "Uncle Allan, whatever does she mean?"

The class laughed and began to ask questions, which became the focus of our discussion of communication that day. In days following that discussion, some students said that the things we talked about had been a perspective-changing event for them.

= = =

At my office door one afternoon appeared a student I had not met before. He closed the door behind him and explained that he had an unusual concern and that from what he had heard of my experiences, perhaps I could help him.

He was African American, adopted by a white family in a northern state who lived in a town with no African Americans. He grew up with no contact with any African Americans. Now, to broaden his experiences, he had come south to attend college. He explained that he was experiencing culture-shock, as some African Americans he met expected him to know certain things, have certain perspectives, talk in certain ways, and have certain behaviors, which he did not comprehend.

He said that he had heard I lived in an African-American neighborhood, had taught at two African-American colleges, associated daily for years with African Americans. Perhaps, he said, I was the one who could help him understand so he could make a more successful transition into his new circumstances.

We began an event-by-event review of what he was experiencing and explored the ways of escaping categories.

I emphasized how being content with one's unique self and life circumstances gives each of us a rich background from which others could learn. He gained excitement from the prospects of reframing his insights and helping others to do so as well.

= = =

Albert II was flying home for Christmas break from MIT where he attended school. In high school he had said one day, "I don't want to just be Albert the Second (Albert II) any more." We asked what he wanted instead. He thought intently for a moment and said, "I want to be Albert the Great." Thus christened that day, we continued in the family to refer to him that way, which occasionally brought questioning glances from others.

His father and I and my son went out to meet him at the airport on his return from MIT for the holiday. Another professor from UALR was also there waiting to meet his incoming passenger. In our conversation, he asked who we were meeting. My son said it was his cousin, attending MIT.

My colleague remarked that it was so crowded at the airport, we might have difficulty in locating the people we were waiting for. My son replied that we would have no problem, for his cousin had grown to six feet eight inches in height, and always could be located above the other heads of the crowd.

When the passengers were disembarking, the crowd was dense, and the professor repeated his remarks about locating people. But indeed, there was Albert II, head and shoulders above the rest, clearly visible. My son said that there he was, just like he had predicted. The professor said that he saw no one taller than the others. My son said to look there, at the person in the red jacket. The professor finally focused on the red jacket and blurted out, "He can't be your cousin, he's b....." But before the word was finished, his mind switched gears and he said, "he's b... tall, very TALL."

At this point my son ran forward, and he and his cousin embraced. My son grabbed Albert II by the hand and led him over to meet the professor, introducing him as Albert the Great, which brought another look of surprise from the professor, who shook his hand, cast a glance at me, and said, "Yes, he really is taller than the rest of the family."

That same evening at the airport, an unrelated but interesting incident occurred as we were standing waiting at the baggage claim for the suitcases to appear. Three girls of college age who were also waiting, kept looking over at Albert II, pointing and talking to each other. Finally they came over and asked him, "Are you *somebody*? And what team do you play for?"

24

Albert and I both enjoyed music. He had studied piano and, as a youth, had played at three different churches in McComb. I had also studied piano in grade school and played in the junior orchestra and in a dance band in high school. He had for years collected recordings of operas and had built an extensive collection. He tried never to miss the Metropolitan Opera broadcasts on Saturday afternoons.

We wanted to attend the Arkansas Symphony Orchestra concerts and purchased season tickets, for ourselves and our wives and a fifth person. She was an elderly music teacher who loved music, but could no longer drive and had no one to take her to concerts. So we picked her up for each occasion and enjoyed sharing her experience of being energized by the performances.

At first, it was still unusual enough to see people out interracially together so that each of us had people approach us at various times saying they had seen us with the others and wondering how we knew each other.

We and our wives also began to attend the Arkansas Repertory Theatre (REP) when it had newly opened in the space that had been an old store on Kavanaugh Boulevard. We followed it, with our four season tickets, as the REP moved to an old church building in east Little Rock, and then to its location on Main Street. Early on, as with the symphony, we individually received questions about the "other family" we were with.

The REP, aiming to diversify its audience, diversified its board, asking Albert to serve on it.

As the Weekend Theater was developing, both Albert and I were asked to serve on its board, which we agreed to, and we attended every performance.

To these and other performances Albert tried continually to encourage those to attend who would contribute to the diversity of the audiences, now open to everyone.

As we attended any kind of public presentation, we observed and talked about the amount and kinds of diversity represented. As time passed, we took notice of the changes.

25

An international conference took us to Singapore. We continued to have people from the sessions and on the street ask us about racial conditions in the United States and the unusualness of seeing "diverse Americans" traveling together.

In Thailand, a conference itinerary took us to a location for an elephant ride. We both could fit on the elephant's back behind the mahout, who guided the animal, on the indescribable ride of swaying back and forth with each step. We afterwards found that a photograph was taken of each elephant and its passengers as a token of the unusual experience.

Unusual experiences were related to conferences in most locations. In Ecuador we found ourselves standing with one foot on either side of the equator.

Just six hundred and fifty miles off the coast of Ecuador lie the Galapagos Islands. With inhabitants on only five of the 12 islands, which are the peaks of mountains rising as much as 10,000 feet from the ocean floor, this wildlife sanctuary is an area that contributed to

Charles Darwin's formulation of the theory of evolution in *The Origin of Species*.

We walked the paths on the islands, following the scientists who described the flora and fauna and the interconnectedness and significance of each.

= = =

We began to study information about the Trail of Tears, realizing that one of its major routes came through Little Rock. The term referred to the forced relocation of Native American tribes from eastern parts of the United States following the Indian Removal Act of 1830. Tens of thousands of Native Americans traveled along various routes to the west, including the Cherokee, Choctaw, Muscogee, Creek, and Seminole tribes.

Albert and I found the study had personal connections. He had Choctaw heritage and I, Cherokee heritage. Mirth emerged when friends, finding out we had these two tribal connections, joked that it was remarkable we got along so well, being from two different tribes.

The non-profit Trail of Tears Association (TOTA) supports efforts to preserve locations and information about the various routes of the trail, with state chapters in Alabama, Arkansas, Georgia, Illinois, Kentucky, Missouri, North Carolina, Oklahoma, and Tennessee. We found it interesting to learn that the national office of the Trail of Tears Association was located about a mile from our neighborhood.

We began to attend state chapter meetings and also the national meetings, always held in a city through which the trail passed. Among the attendees interested in the preservation of trail-related locations and information were individuals who came from European and African backgrounds, and it also attracted participants from Native American tribes. From this mix of people came a rich flow of discussion both in the conference sessions and the between-session interactions.

Recurring humor at the conferences included, as in the title of one session, "Why Indians Don't Use Twenty-Dollar Bills." Because, of course, that bill carries the likeness of Andrew Jackson, the president who gave the Indian removal order. Cherokee lawyers had fought against the removal all the way to the Supreme Court, and the court ruled in their favor. Jackson defied the court and went ahead with the removal.

At that session, when a Native American referred to not using $20 bills, there was another Native American nearby who came forth with, "I'll help you out, just give your $20 bills to me." That routine was repeated at numerous occasions.

At early TOTA meetings, even with the diverse attendance, people noted that people of diverse backgrounds usually did not come together, and Albert and I would be asked about how we had met.

= = =

We were members of the International Listening Association. The ILA was a professional organization to explore and promote the benefits of effective listening. Communication associations usually focused on the presentation of messages, while the ILA focused on the other half of the process, the receiving and understanding of what was presented. The annual meetings were held in a variety of locations, both within and outside of the United States.

I was presenting a research paper on Listening by Personality Inventory, when we went to the ILA conference in Seattle. The presentations were creative and fascinating. At an evening session, the program was interrupted by one of the coordinators. He said that at this same conference hotel where we were meeting, the cast and crew of the television series *Northern Exposure* were also staying. They had just returned from their day of filming and, walking through the lobby, saw listed the activities of the International Listening Association. Never having heard of it before, and feeling that the study of listening was a remarkable undertaking, they asked if they could come into the evening activity to "see what these people were like" and "what they were doing."

Since many of the ILA participants were watchers of the quirky television series and understood how the group that created that show might find the ILA to be equally quirky, the group responded with a collective "yes." In came the cast and crew who were invited to the stage. What followed was a question and answer session going from *Northern Exposure* to ILA and back again.

One of the cast laughed as he said that we had discovered their little secret, that the show's fictional town of Cicely, Alaska, was not in Alaska at all, but near Seattle.

Another cast member looked at the ILA audience and asked, "Are you listening?"

26

The Meals-On-Wheels program enlists volunteers to take hot meals prepared at a central kitchen to the homes of older individuals who could not continue independent living without assistance. Albert and I paired up on a route.

At times, we might be among the few people, or the only persons, who the individual would see during the day. Friendships grew up over the weeks and months and years.

When one apartment-dwelling lady asked if we ever went to see the plays at the REP, and we said yes, she invited us in to talk about how much she missed her "old life" when she and friends attended as many of the plays, concerts, and special performances in town as possible. But those people had died and she was not mobile enough to attend any more, and she desperately missed the events.

So Albert and I started getting an extra program for all of the performances we attended and took them to her. She would ask us in to sit and talk about each one in turn. We left the programs with her, which she said she read several times each. She called in neighbors from other apartments and shared the stories of the performances with them.

As we brought in a batch of programs one day, she said that she was now "experiencing vicariously" all these events and that it was as if she had "been revived" in the continued excitement of each discussion.

At one house, where a widow lived alone, we rang the doorbell and could see through the small pane of glass in the front door as she struggled from her chair on the far side of the room, stepped forward and fell to the floor. The door was locked, but we saw her start to crawl with great effort toward the door, finally reaching the door knob from her recumbent position on the floor. We entered, phoned her son, and waited until he arrived.

A man who lived alone also invited us in each time to sit and talk a while. Besides food, he had other needs that he felt frustrated not being able to take care of. He had laundry to be done and no one to take it to the cleaners. So we took it and picked it up and continued the process.

We delivered two meals to one household where a brother and sister, after both of their spouses died, moved in together to help each other. They had owned a downtown Little Rock business and were deeply interested in what was going on downtown.

The sister invited us in and wanted to know our backgrounds. Each time thereafter she expected us to come in and sit at her breakfast counter with her. She would have a stack of notes and clippings of things she wanted to ask about.

Since she was unable to get out to visit her former business location, she wanted updates on what it looked like now. So we would take pictures of it to bring to her. She would invite friends in to meet us to join in our conversations.

She lived on the edge of our delivery area. One day the brother and sister's names were not on our delivery sheet. They had been taken off of our route and added to the adjoining route. When we finished our deliveries, we went on by their home anyway. She said she was overjoyed that we came because she didn't know how to get in touch with us and she wanted to continue our conversations. So each time, after our other deliveries were completed, even though someone else had delivered the meals, we circled around and spent our time together. When her brother died, we stood with her at the graveside service. On a subsequent visit to her home, she said, "Thank you for bringing the world to me."

Then there was our lady in the "birdcage." That is what she called her small garage apartment. The garage stood several feet behind a spacious home where she had previously lived. But needing income, she had rented out the big house and moved into the small space. When cabinet doors stuck, hinges were loose, or something was on a shelf out of her reach as her abilities diminished, she would ask us for help and called us her "rescuers."

When I appeared with the meal by myself on a day when Albert had a meeting to attend, she added another word to the terms that people had used to refer to the two of us. When she answered the door, she looked on both sides of me and back along the driveway and said, "Where is he? Where's your copilot?" So copilot joined terms others had used such as civil rights brothers, Arkansas twins, brothers from different mothers, the daring duo.

A man on our route invited us in to "sit a spell" and talk about what was going on in the nation and world. He said he looked forward to these conversations so much he didn't know what he would do without them. He invited people over so we could meet them.

One lady said, "All right, you two bring me meals, and now I've just got to get you each a meal." So she asked us to come back after we had delivered the other meals, pick her up, so we could drive to her favorite catfish restaurant that she could no longer get to, and we had a catfish lunch together.

A woman explained that when growing up, she was the only one in her family that favored integration, the rest being outspoken segregationists, which, she said, isolated her somewhat from them. She took hold of our hands and said that she could not begin to tell us how much it meant to her for us to deliver her meals and become like part of a new family for her.

Another person lived alone in a large house on a busy corner. On warm days, on her front porch, she would set up a small table with three chairs. She prepared the table with a single setting of a linen napkin and actual silverware, a crystal glass, and a flower in a small vase. When we brought her meal, she placed it on the table, asked us to sit down and hold hands in the little circle of three as she asked the blessing of the food, and then thanked us as she began to dine.

As one of the ladies grew more feeble and was making plans to move into a nursing home, she made us promise before her transition that we would come and visit her. When we went, she joked, "Where's my meal?"

Another of the people who enjoyed jokes asked if there was any Meals-On-Wheels humor. We repeated the riddle that had been passed around among some of the meal deliverers. Question: "What does a cat call a roller-skating rink for mice?" Answer: "Meals on wheels."

Some of those on the route no longer had people left to celebrate their birthdays. When we discovered this, we would appear at their doors with a birthday cake.

One lady, who had come to Little Rock from New Orleans after a hurricane had damaged much in that city and who referred to herself as a "refugee," still felt her identity to be there. When Mardi Gras approached, she decorated her apartment door with Mardi Gras masks and beads. We located a local bakery that made King Cakes for Mardi Gras, bought one, and took it to her. She said that really helped to bring the spirit of the season to her. The next week, she told us she had invited people from neighboring apartments to come and partake of the cake with her and have a Mardi Gras party. We brought her a cake every year thereafter.

27

When the Olympics were held in Atlanta, the Olympic Torch was being carried through cities across the country, with local persons invited to carry it for a distance and pass it to the next waiting person. Plans were made for the torch to be carried through Little Rock, and Albert was invited to be one of the torch bearers.

On the day of the event, family and friends stood on the sides of the street to cheer him on. He received the flaming torch from the person preceding him. Days later, a heavy tubular package was delivered to his home. It was a torch for him to keep, just like the one he had carried along the street.

= = =

Watching an evening newscast on a major network, the news anchor announced the next international story and switched to the correspondent covering it. I especially enjoyed seeing that correspondent because he was a friend I had first met during my freshman year in college at Denison University in Ohio. He had grown up in New York City.

In college, Hal Walker and I had had long discussions about futures and possible jobs and plans. He had several interests and wanted to do something "groundbreaking," to be the first African American in some field that could open the way for others.

When Albert and I were in New York City for a national conference, I called Hal, and he asked where we were at that moment and identified a place nearby where he could meet us.

He had gone to work in television, and write-ups identified him as "the first black correspondent hired by CBS News." He had also worked for ABC News, at their London bureau and as bureau chief in Bonn. He was equally interested in our episodes in civil rights activities.

= = =

The Tuskegee Airmen became respected for the accomplishments they made under difficult conditions during World War II. One of the airmen was Albert's uncle. He not only flew in the early years but chose to remain in service and make the air force a full career.

He and his wife lived on the coast of South Carolina. Albert and I would drive the distance to see them a few times each year. In the time spent with them, it seemed that any subject that came up, the uncle had a story related to it concerning his experiences in the air force.

We heard the stories of how President Roosevelt had given the order to create a "black flying unit," subsequently located at Tuskegee, Alabama. We heard how Eleanor Roosevelt had visited the base and gained publicity for the project when it was reported that she "flew with a pilot of color." We learned of the enthusiasm the newly trained pilots had when assigned a new aircraft, the P-51 Mustang, and how the tails were painted red for ease of recognition of each other during air battles. The Germans called them Schwarze Vogelmenschen, the Black Bird Men.

At every turn, he explained, they met layers and levels of prejudice. He regaled us with stories of what he encountered and how he dealt with the circumstances. His stories were so extensive that I laughingly suggested that we could open the dictionary to any random page, point to a word, and he would have a story related to it. He thought for only a moment before saying, "Yes!"

He felt that the outstanding performance of the Tuskegee Airmen in such challenging circumstances helped hasten the moment when, after the war ended, President Truman signed Executive Order 9981, which desegregated the United States military.

Later, I obtained a replica leather flight jacket with the words *Tuskegee Airmen* emblazoned on the back along with a colorful rendering of the red-tail plane, with a smaller version on the front. In a restaurant as I was walking toward my table, a seated white customer squinted to read the front of the jacket, stood as I passed by, easily reading the back. From behind me I heard his words, "I don't think so." An African-American clerk in a grocery store looked at it and asked, "Do you still fly those planes?" In a grocery store aisle, two African-American customers followed me, both men reading the back of the jacket, then coming up on either side of me, putting an arm around my shoulders, each raising their other hand in the air, and exclaiming, "Yes!" Exiting a movie theater, a couple stopped me and, pointing to the jacket, asked, "Were you their flight instructor who taught them how to fly?"

= = =

I was asked to teach communication classes for college credit in Arkansas prisons. They arranged to have the three-hour-a-week class on one night instead of spreading it out over three days as on campus.

On the night of my first class in prison, I had driven to the location in the evening following a full day of work on campus. I was led down a long secured corridor to the classroom. As I handed out the syllabus and discussed the overview of the coming class, I asked if there were any questions. One inmate raised his hand and asked, "Have you ever had a captive audience before?" Everyone burst out in laughter.

One of the class members came up to me afterwards and asked if I remembered a student from one of my previous classes on campus. I said that I did, and he explained that it was his sister and that she was excited that he was going to have a chance to benefit from the material that she had so appreciated. He smiled and said, "It's a small world, isn't it."

In addition, I was asked by the Police Academy in Camden to teach communication classes to policemen from across the state. When I worked that into my schedule, I found myself at the same time dealing with classes on campus, in prison, and at the police academy.

It seemed an opportune time to do a semantic study of the perception of these three groups, about themselves and about each of the others. I asked them to write three lists, each a series of 10 words that described their view of themselves and of the other two groups. I shared the responses with each group so they could hear how they perceived themselves and how others perceived them. All three expressed surprise at how incorrectly the others regarded them. That fostered intense and beneficial discussions. It led them to conclude that in each case they were responding to the idea of categories rather that diverse individuals. When I presented the results at communication conferences, the audiences said they found the results fascinating, causing them to think about similar studies they might pursue in their locations.

28

The drive from Little Rock to South Carolina took us through Tennessee, and the city of Jackson, the location of Lane College. We stopped to see those in town we had worked so closely with during the extensive civil rights activities. They kept us posted on the progress being made in education, employment, housing, and other facets of working toward equal opportunities for all.

One of the persons who had been a student when we worked there had since gone on to graduate school and then returned to Lane to teach. In time he became the president of the college and asked us always to stop by when driving through. He would tour us through the campus, pointing out new developments and accomplishments. He credited much of his professional success to the disciplines and insights he gained during our civil rights activities.

Reflecting on that time, he instituted the college's Dr. Martin Luther King Jr. Memorial Celebration and award. He invited us for the celebration and presented Albert with the award to honor him for his leadership and accomplishments.

The efforts for civil rights had many casualties, some almost invisible. Among them were local white citizens who were often the solitary ones in their area to speak out for equal rights, only to be ostracized by the wrath of their peers. We sought out one of those men to see how he had fared as the years had passed.

When he had tried to explain to his friends that he felt all people deserved equal opportunities, their retaliation took many forms. They boycotted his business until he lost it. They excluded his wife from any of her social circles and would not visit with nor speak to her. Their church excluded them from all activities, saying he was defying the will of God, which was racial separation, and they were no longer welcome in the house of worship. His children were regularly bullied and beaten up by other children at school with no intervention from school officials. His wife, unable to withstand the poverty, exclusion from all social contact, and the endangerment of the children, divorced him.

He did not want to leave town and give injustice another victory. As one person described him, "He became like a ghost of the person he used to be."

= = =

There were events that the Porters and Wards celebrated together. My wife's birthday and Albert's birthday occurred within five days of each other in December, so the families would go out to dinner to celebrate both birthdays at the same time.

Coincidently, Albert's wife's birthday and my birthday were two days apart in January. So the same course of action took place as our families went out for a single dinner to celebrate both birthdays.

Not uncommonly, in restaurants that would bring out pieces of cake with a lighted candle and servers would sing happy birthday, we would attract attention in the earlier years for our unusual combination. We talked about how we looked forward to the day, as society changed, that such blending would become so commonplace that it would attract no special attention.

We joined together for Thanksgiving dinners and Christmas dinners at one or the other's home, and invited people to join us who had no one else to be with on those holidays.

29

At an international communication conference in Spain, Albert and I found ourselves hearing discourses on ethnic differences in various parts of the world, including ongoing tensions where our conference was being held in the north of the country. Conference field trips took us high in the Pyrenees Mountains into Basque country to speak with persons of that ethnicity. The mountain chain extended more than 300 miles from the Bay of Biscay to the Mediterranean, forming a barrier between the Iberian Peninsula and the rest of Europe.

There were discussions about how the Basque language was not related to any of the surrounding European family of languages, suggesting a culture that predated the others. As migration of the Indo-European speakers came in, the Basque ancestors found refuge in the mountains, maintaining their culture and language.

Some of our stops included restaurants to sample the Basque foods along with the questions and conversations. Even there, Albert and I received questions about the conditions in the United States and our activities in civil rights.

The Basques had contacted the Solomon R. Guggenheim Foundation about building a museum in Bilbao, the capital of the province of Biscay in the autonomous community of the Basque Country. When completed, the building was an artwork in itself, bright with titanium, glass, and limestone. We walked its halls filled with extraordinary art.

Our conference travel in Spain took us on to Picos De Europa National Park in the Pyrenees, where we walked its winding trails and rode the lift to one of the highest peaks, the dangling carriage swaying over spectacular valleys below.

We continued onward south in Spain, talking with historians about the effect on the country in 1492 when Queen Isabella and King Ferdinand forced the members of the Spanish Jewish communities to either convert to Catholicism, leave the country, or be killed. We talked to families who said they were descendants of some of those families who stayed, converted outwardly, but in private continued their traditional practices as much as possible.

We ended up in Madrid. There, as in other places to which we traveled, we enjoyed walking the streets to get a feeling for the locations. We found surprises on the way, as when we investigated a large building along the boulevard and realized we had encountered the Museo del Prado. The building was designed in 1785 and opened to the public for the first time in 1819. There we viewed the works of Francisco de Goya, Diego Velazquez, Titian, Peter Paul Rubens, Hieronymus Bosch, and many others.

$$= = =$$

A conference in Costa Rica led to a connection to what we had learned in Spain. Talking with residents there, it turned out many were descendants of the Jewish population driven out of Spain. These settlers differed greatly from the crude conquistadors and other gold hunters. They constituted one of the most educated and learned groups ever to resettle in the Americas. One person told us that it was because of this founding that the country currently had one of the highest education levels in the world, and that it was no coincidence that the country had abolished its army in 1948, transferring the military budget to the education system.

This provided a context for the United Nations General Assembly to pass a resolution establishing an international commission, collaborating with the government of Costa Rica to organize a remarkable institution, the University for Peace, UPEACE.

As Albert and I toured its campus, the administrator explained how countries have military schools which teach how to wage war. Why, then, should there not be a school which would consider peace, not as the passive absence of war, but as an active goal of how to wage peace.

The students, from various countries, pursue their courses toward master's degrees and in doctoral programs. UPEACE has partnership arrangements with other institutions in many parts of the world. We talked with students and heard their passion for actively learning and working to build peace. They asked of our participation in civil rights projects, and likened what we had actively done to bring diverse people together to build understanding and cooperation as a parallel to what they were doing.

They explained how their activities are aimed at developing skills of leadership including intercultural communication, negotiation, conflict resolution, and team-building. They asked us for examples of activities we had used to promote these ideas and skills.

One of them said, "I had little hope for the world and its conflicts until I heard of UPEACE and came here and met others who felt like I did, realizing that we can each make a difference in the right direction." They explained how they have a strong alumni network to support each other, working in places of conflict, with non-governmental agencies, in academic and inter-governmental institutions. Then they smiled and said, "But since you're here, now you must go trek into the jungle to see things you've never seen before." And we did.

A biologist and a botanist guided us through jungle pathways, describing the elements of an ecosystem of plants and animals. We saw insects that had taken on the textures and colors of the plants they lived on, and watched snakes dangling from tree limbs. We rode an aerial tram suspended from cables running through the treetops of the rain forest, as the guides called attention to nests on branches and hollows in trunks housing a variety of creatures. We saw birds with fanciful plummage that produced a range of trills, caws, and calls. The guides led us to brooks and streams to view fish and reptiles and frogs in a rainbow of colors.

30

Many classes in high school and college touch on the civil rights activities, relating to history, communication, psychology, sociology, and other areas. Albert and I were asked to come to classes and speak and answer questions. Students frequently said that reading about the civil rights activities in textbooks somehow seemed distant and impersonal until they heard the firsthand accounts and how individuals were affected.

Many times when they went home following those discussions, they would tell their families about our stories. They found that this opened up memories of family members who shared their own stories with their children, who then brought them back to share with their class. This process generated more questions, and Albert and I were often asked to return to the class to participate in this next level of discussion.

We met so many students this way that we would encounter individuals again in some store or other public place. When they would greet us, what usually followed was a continuation of some aspect of the classroom discussion or some specific episode from their own families.

When one of them said, "It's a shame there isn't somewhere we could go to study peace." And our response led right back to Costa Rica.

= = =

A conference took us to Sweden in the land of the midnight sun. The daylight lasted 24 hours a day as the sun rolled around above the horizon continually.

At the conference, questions arose from those from other locations who were accustomed to light days and dark nights, where even in the shorter hours of light some people experienced the Seasonal Affective Disorder (SAD). One person asked, "Why do people in other parts of the world experience the SAD syndrome during longer periods of darkness but people here don't, with weeks of darkness?" Our conference hosts laughed and explained that the SAD syndrome had its effect on their population as well, in the extreme, some people having a hard time getting up at all during the darkness.

The conference sessions were interspersed with side trips to historic sites, museums, castles, and seaports. Some were surprised to realize that the city of Stockholm is spread across 13 islands or of Stockholm's archipelago of more than 20,000 islands across Lake Malaren toward the Baltic Sea.

The historians guiding us through these places took pleasure in our responses when, with a casual gesture, they would point toward buildings and say something like, "Oh, by the way, that was Ingrid Bergman's home." They would then proceed with the stories related to the building.

= = =

As time passed and conditions improved, local areas began to change their attitude toward the civil rights leaders, once viewed as trouble makers, now regarded as agents of positive social change. Albert, who had previously had his life threatened, was invited back to Jackson to be honored for his major contributions to the city's advancement.

He had no interest in the attention personally, but rejoiced in the changes that such an event represented in the transformation of social structure. He spoke at the celebrations, praising the changes that had been made and congratulating everyone on the contributions they had made.

My department at Ohio University held a commemoration for the anniversary of my graduation as their first Ph.D. graduate. They flew me back for the celebratory series of events. In the ceremonies, I inwardly recalled the statements from my advisor that they should never have wasted their fellowship funds or time on me, while their current focus was praising that very use of the communications training to contribute to the advancement of equality.

= = =

When, years before, our neighborhood of University Park had opened for housing and Albert and I had selected lots there, and the other families were moving in, we helped to start a neighborhood association that could meet and consider the safety and well-being of the community.

He suggested that the neighborhood have an annual picnic to help people socialize, to recognize achievements, and to increase for the children a sense of having an extended family. Then he offered his back yard for the event. Since we had fenced our lots together, we had ample space.

He had also built a swimming pool, not only for his children and mine, but opened it up in the summertime for all the children of the community, with the written approval of their parents. At the picnics, the pool was also available.

We secured an outdoor grill and spent a couple of days setting up tables and chairs, asking everyone to bring additional lawn chairs with them. People arrived and talked, mixed, mingled, and shared stories. Newcomers each year were warmly welcomed. If questions had arisen at our periodic neighborhood meetings about some aspect of community life that needed outside answers, we invited those who could respond, as when police officers came to address safety issues.

Albert was elected president of the neighborhood association and saw to it that a regular newsletter was distributed to keep people informed. He and I would deliver them to every home in the neighborhood.

The youth who grew up attending the picnics and swimming regularly in his pool expressed their appreciation for the kindness. When many of those were college age and beyond, they gathered one summer from their diverse locations and reminisced about their growing up in the neighborhood.

After they had met, one of them came to express their collective gratitude. He said they all agreed that the friendship of the two families had a lasting impact on them. "It made a difference in so many ways we cannot even describe, and we wanted to thank you both for making that difference and for being like extended family to us."

Soon after, another youth stopped me on the street and said that when he and the others saw the problems people had with each other, our two families had given them not just hope for the future but "a living example of it."

31

The New Zealand author of text material on the United States civil rights period asked to come to see us. He wanted firsthand information and was interviewing those he considered key figures in the movement.

He not only taught courses in New Zealand about the civil rights era, but wanted to arrange a substantial field trip for his students after they had studied the material. So he brought his students across the ocean to tour different locations in the U.S. and to talk with people with whom he had made contact.

Albert and I sat in a circle with the eager and well-versed students and answered questions. We discussed what could be learned from the U.S. civil rights movement about human interaction and principles of social change that could apply to individuals and movements everywhere. The author and teacher said our stories would be included in his published materials.

A year later, we received a communication from the teacher saying he was coming again with another class and asked us to plan another day of discussion.

The students expressed what their studies and experiences meant to them. They said they now understood that the civil rights movement in the United States had an impact on other countries globally in their own social changes.

= = =

Albert and I were invited to chair sessions at an international conference in Australia. We journeyed to Brisbane, staying at the downtown conference hotel with the sessions being held at the nearby university campus. Between sessions, we were approached by local participants who talked about the history of the relationship between the Euro-Australians and the Aboriginal peoples. They asked many questions about our experiences in American civil rights activities that could relate to them.

Even walking daily between hotel and university, there were people who stopped us to express their curiosity about conditions in America and how we could have even met there under the conditions of segregation.

= = =

To gather intercultural information in Peru, Albert and I walked the streets of Lima, surrounded by evidence of the confrontation of cultures when the Spanish invaders met the resident Incas. We talked about how the conflict of cultures, ethnicities, and races have repeated themselves over and over around the earth, like echoes passing through the centuries and generations of people categorizing others and treating them as lesser than themselves.

We heard the stories of how Francisco Pizarro, after forays in Mexico and Panama, came to Peru. The Incan leader, Atahualpa, resisted the newcomers. In 1532, Pizarro captured him, set a ransom, which was to fill a room with gold. Once this was accomplished, Pizarro broke his promise of release and proceeded to murder the Incan.

We proceeded on to Cuzco, the ancient Incan capital. Pizarro had entered soon after killing Atahualpa and proceeded to proclaim the establishment of his own city, on the top of the Incan one. As we walked the streets of Cuzco, we saw evidence everywhere of the foundations of Incan structures with a visible line of demarcation where the Spanish buildings were constructed on top of them. But we heard the stories of how even conquerors have conflicts and received the treatment they had exhibited. Pizarro and his fellow conquistador, Diego de Almagro, argued, climaxing in the Battle of Las Salinas when Almagro was killed. Subsequently Almagro's son killed Pizarro.

About 70 miles from Cuzco is the "lost city of the Incas," Machu Picchu. We traveled there, hearing stories from the archeologists along the way. Built by the Incas before the arrival of the Europeans, it was never found by them, perched at an altitude of more than 8,000 feet, not visible from the valley floor. Deserted and covered with jungle overgrowth, it remained until 1911 for Hiram Bingham of Connecticut to rediscover and introduce it to the outside world.

There, walkways and stairways pass among some 200 buildings, the straw roofs of which are long gone, with much of the stonework walls still intact. We walked among the ruins with explanations from the anthropologists about the findings that suggested what the various areas were once used for.

Previously at the Lima airport, we had noticed a group of people gathered in the waiting area off to the side making music. In Cuzco we encountered them again, once more hearing their music in various places but not to any particular audience. Traveling with them to Machu Picchu, we asked about their music. They were "inspirational musicians" made up of individuals who had discovered each other through social media. They did not perform previously-composed pieces, but felt that various locations had a "spirit" that could use them as instruments.

Accordingly they, who were employed at a variety of jobs, met during vacations and holidays to travel to various places, turning on a recorder, gathering around it, allowing spontaneous inspiration to move them to create music on the spot, captured by the recording. The goal of this journey was Macho Picchu, where they looked forward to what this "sacred place" would channel through them.

They gathered in the lengthening shadows of the late afternoon in the remnant of the old city plaza. We listened as the first person began with a few notes, joined quickly by a second, until the whole group was producing music never heard before, a shimmering sound to which, as another listener noted, the ghosts of ancient inhabitants might be dancing.

= = =

In Peru, when Albert and I had entered a restaurant among many other customers, a small child, seated at a table, looking at the crowd, singled him out, smiling at him, laughing, and holding out his arms to be picked up. Albert picked him up, hugged him while spinning around, and returned him to his chair. The whole table smiled, one saying, "He likes you!"

A small instance in itself, but I had seen this repeated in Turkey, Japan, Egypt, France, and many other countries, and places in the United States. There was something that attracted children of all backgrounds to him. Occasionally children would ask their family if they could come to our table to eat with us. One even asked to sit in his lap while eating. Others asked their families to take their picture with him.

He had said, many times, in our presentations about civil rights that he felt especially concerned about the children and their well-being, wanting them to be free from the prejudices of their ancestors and free to be with each other. He said they all were our children and needed to feel the love from their whole human family. Something in his compassion for them communicated itself, and they responded.

32

Calls came to consult with various groups who had concerns about a variety of issues regarding diversity. The members of an association of white ministers felt that, as other facets of society were integrating, maybe their churches should do something.

When we met with them, they explained that they did not know what to do to diversify and wanted help and direction as to how to go about it, step by step. We met for months as they cautiously considered options. Several of them, on broaching the possibilities with their congregations, were met with some of their members responding that if the minister continued in this direction, they would either leave the church or try to fire him.

Some backed off, saying they would let time take its course and see what happened. Others approached ministers of black churches to see if they could start "visitations" with each other, in services, in socials, or other events. White ministers expressed surprise when a few of the black ministers told them frankly that they did not want any mixing. They feared that some of their members might be lured to the white churches, and they would be left with smaller congregations and lower income.

We discussed how our group of ministers needed to work first with their own congregations so that as steps were taken the members would support the activities. We developed workshops to help accomplish this task.

= = =

As integration began, a call came from managers of housing units, saying that they needed help with the people living in the units to accept the new arrivals that were bringing diversity. They wanted us to conduct workshops with those residents to prepare them for changes.

They also wanted the current occupants to have preparation for the workshops, suggesting that they needed to be visited individually to talk with them to see what their concerns might be. It took weeks for us to set up all of the appointments and visitations and the workshops. They reported that the subsequent transitions went peacefully.

= = =

Diversity training can apply to many kinds of situations. A call came from a national company headquartered in a northeastern state, which had an emerging problem with a high-level executive. He had made what the board considered unacceptable, demeaning, condescending statements about women. The board was faced with either replacing or "rehabilitating" him.

They gave him the option of either leaving the company or of flying into Little Rock for a series of sessions for "personal therapy in diversity acceptance," which, if "successful," would permit him to continue in his position. He accepted the latter.

Working with him, the basic need was to change his stereotyped concept and replace the category of female with the inclusive idea of men and women as human individuals. With his initial resentment of even being questioned, he flew in several weeks for the day-long sessions. Each time, it was possible to take examples from the reframing of racial attitudes, which he understood more easily, and apply them to his situation.

He found the reframing of perspective he was undergoing "transformative and life-changing," and discovered he could apply it to other stereotyped concepts in himself which he began to discover. He was able to return to his position and hoped he could now help others in whom he might recognize the symptoms that he had personally dealt with.

= = =

Another company from the west coast called. They specialized in conducting inspirational workshops across the country to train and motivate people in all lines of business. The people in their organization who interacted with the public were the individual workshop presenters. As diversity in businesses was increasing, the company owners had a concern with the ability of their presenters to deal with these changes in a positive manner. If they did not, the popularity of their sessions might decrease and thus their income be reduced.

They could train their presenters in the workshop content, but the management wanted outside help in evaluating how well the presenters dealt with diversity and inclusiveness, and how well they connected with the variety of people in their workshops.

They wanted to fly us to cities where the workshops were being presented, sit through the workshops, and take extensive notes on all of the interactions. Our goal was to identify any aspects that needed help, develop strategies to assist the presenters, and have sessions with them to accomplish that improvement.

At one workshop in New Orleans, after finishing with the evaluation and exiting onto the street, the surprise was to find crowds along the walkways. So concentrated had the attention been on the workshop, it had been easy to forget that this was Mardi Gras and a parade was coming down the street.

= = =

Medical centers also called for help with diversity training for their staffs. Not only racial, but ethnic and gender problems arose. As the tradition of male doctors and female nurses was changing as more women became doctors and more men became nurses, individual prejudices surfaced. One institution called for help. They explained that some of the male doctors refused to speak directly to female doctors or to male nurses. Instead they would give orders to female nurses to pass on to the others, even when the others were standing there beside them.

In another medical facility which was hiring increasing numbers of doctors and nurses from other countries, ethnic prejudices from those regions surfaced around the operating table, with instances of these professionals cursing at each other during the operation. The intervention was to bring them all together and begin the process of having them separate their coworkers from their ethnic classifications and begin to deal with them as individual human beings. When I had asked them how many felt they had experienced others reacting to them prejudicially, nearly all of them raised their hands.

In these instances, we could draw on examples from racial pre-judgments and discuss how lessons could be drawn from those examples that applied to solving their situations.

In follow-up communications, some of the participants expressed their gratitude, explaining that they felt much better within themselves after understanding and dealing with the hurtful preconceptions that they had inherited from family and acquaintances. One said that she realized she had been carrying around "a load of faulty assumptions" that had been "dumped" on her since childhood that were damaging everything she did, and she felt she had been freed from those at last.

= = =

Albert and I were invited to speak at a conference in Athens, Greece. The international gathering provided opportunities to consult with people from around the world. We heard the stories of the various kinds of discrimination in each society, by looks, gender, class, caste, wealth, age, world views, occupation, and a host of others.

But the pattern was always the same: assumptions were made about people because of the category in which they were viewed.

We made notations about many of these examples to use in our future workshops in diversity training. We had found that by using examples from outside of the participants' region, they could see the pattern more clearly and less emotionally. Then we could more easily help them to see that same pattern in their own circumstances.

Opportunities were provided to visit the ancient sites in Athens. Walking near the Parthenon, conversations turned to the positive inheritance from the Greeks and other cultures as well as the negative aspects. It was noted how important it is for individuals to review their inherited traditions and consciously evaluate what to keep and what to discard.

The conference opportunities took us outside the city and across Greece. Looking out on the plains in one location, we noticed the remains of an ancient settlement were visible. Unlike others we had seen that had walls around them for protection from attacks, these seemed to have none. We asked our anthropologist-leader about that, and she responded that there was a time before the recorded battles in history when a time of peace seemed evident by the lack of fortifications. But when diverse people with different ways of doing and viewing things began to encounter each other, conflicts and fortifications increased.

We discussed how those kinds of confrontations, with changing groups, had continued through the centuries. We could see how they connected with the contemporary civil and human rights issues of today.

Boat travel from the conference took us to Crete, the largest of the Greek Islands. We walked the sites remaining of the Minoan civilization of 5,000 years ago. In Knossos at the Palace of Minos, the murals provided a view of how the ancients portrayed their world, as the anthropologists, in their descriptions, linked the past and present.

Then onward our group traveled by boat to another location of the ancient Minoan civilization, the island of Santorini . Our archeologist said we were about to visit the site that is probably the source of the story of Atlantis. The island, he explained, is what remains of what was once a larger volcanic island, which produced one of the largest volcanic eruptions in recorded history. Taking place some 3,500 years ago, the enormous blast left a huge hole, a water-filled caldera, several miles across, with just an arc of land at the edges remaining as the present islands, the largest being Santorini. The huge wave produced by the explosion swept through the Aegean and Mediterranean Seas, wiping out many shore settlements including those on Crete, and probably bringing an end to the Minoan civilization.

Arriving at Santorini, we walked down into the excavations begun in the 1960s. The excavators were uncovering streets, walls, buildings several-levels high, pipes for hot and cold running water, all buried in volcanic ash for more than 3,000 years, with most of the remains yet to be uncovered. With a sweeping gesture as we walked along the ancient streets, the anthropologist said, "Atlantis!"

Our group journeyed on to Turkey, to Ephesus. There we heard the stories of St. Paul's imprisonment, and saw the site of one of the seven wonders of the ancient world— the Temple of Artemis—completed about 550 B.C. The ancient theater had an estimated capacity of 25,000 people, thought to be the largest outdoor theater of the ancient world.

Istanbul was replete with sites. We were told it included more than 400 mosques. The Blue Mosque from the 17th century is the only one with six minarets, where sound and light shows are held. At St. Sophia, we heard exclamations of awe from those viewing it.

Topkapi Palace brought visitors to look at its treasures, and we heard many of them describing their first familiarity with it from the movie of the same name.

The bridge across the Bosphorus between the two parts of the city join more than the city. They link two continents, Europe and Asia. Visitors comment that at the middle of the bridge they can stand on two continents at once.

Away from our conference associates during unscheduled time, Albert and I proceeded with our enjoyment of walking unfamiliar streets to see the places and people. Realizing it was lunch time, we entered a restaurant off the beaten path. A group at a table across the way were speaking loudly enough for us to overhear the inflection of their voices, and there was something strangely familiar about their sound. Could it be? Albert and I approached them, and sure enough, it was a group from Arkansas. We all laughed at the improbability of meeting others from Arkansas at an out-of-the-way restaurant in Istanbul.

33

When a long-time friend of ours with whom I worked at the university was moving from Arkansas to New Mexico, Albert and I helped her load the rental truck. We drove the truck westward while she drove her car.

Along a stretch of highway just over the New Mexico border, with miles between buildings and signs indicating how far it was to the next service station, we stopped for gas at an isolated store. A few travelers, like ourselves, were taking advantage of it before the next deserted stretch of highway.

As we exited the store, a man hailed us in the parking lot and said, "Hey, wait up. You know, now that things are changing, there are young people from different racial backgrounds who are getting to know each other. But you guys, you are from a generation where that just didn't happen. How on earth did you hook up?" And under the desert sun, we responded to his long flow of questions. Finally he said, "My God! You are among the civil rights peaceful warriors who made it possible for the next generation and their children to get to where we are today."

And he put an arm around each of us and said, "Thank you, thank you!"

= = =

Referring back to that Native American symbol for friendship of two people starting on opposite sides of a mountain, their paths converging and continuing on side by side, Albert and I had been on that journey together at a particular point in time when our association had been socially unusual. That made it possible, just being together, to have the "teachable moments" and "learning experiences" with people we met who might be able to reframe their experiences and concepts into new more positive perspectives.

Even to be referred to as the dynamic duo, civil rights brothers, Arkansas twins, co-pilots, as well as the civil-righteous brothers was a sign of people seeing our inner unity as more significant than the outer differences.

We had worked to share with others the ideas of viewing people as a collection of inner virtues rather than of outer characteristics. We had sought to assist people to change their perspective from grouping people into categories and reacting with prejudgments about those categories to seeing each person as a unique individual.

We wanted to assist in any way possible to help people find happiness, fulfillment, productivity, peace, companionship, and comfortableness with others. To see these advancements taking place brought joy and purpose to our journey.

About the Author

Dr. Allan Ward is Professor Emeritus of Communication Studies at the University of Arkansas at Little Rock, and a consultant in Intercultural Communication. He has traveled to six continents exploring diverse worldviews. The personal stories from these explorations are included in his book *Beyond the Visible Spectrum*.

He has spoken in Africa, Asia, North and South America, and Europe on communication subjects, including the postmodern perspective. Requests for him to apply this perspective to a distillation of worldviews of those who seek to expand their insight resulted in his book *Postmodern Zen: A Path of Paradox and Process*.

His novel *Lucian* traces the journey of a new college graduate who promptly falls through the cracks between the sound bites, slogans, and social roles that surround him, and he takes up a solitary existence on a worm farm in the desert. His adventures begin as he encounters other desert dwellers on their own quests. Their journeys intertwine and lead to unexpected discoveries.

His novel *Trickster* resulted from his teaching in his Intercultural Communication classes about the mythic

CPSIA information can be obtained
at www.ICGtesting.com
Printed in the USA
FFOW05n1256130514

trickster figures that appear in the stories of cultures around the world. He speculated on what would happen if such a figure appeared today, helping people to "reframe" their experiences and "rewrite" their lives.

As one of the founders of the unlikely "Rhubarb Club" in Arkansas (a place where the plant rarely grows), he wrote and compiled *The Rhubarb Club: Recollections and Recipes*, a whimsical history of the group and an eclectic collection of rhubarb recipes.

He wrote a book of poetry, *Golden Thunder: A Quest for the Inner Poet*, with an usual format, in which a group of fictional poets interact and write, and the reader gets to know them through the poetry attributed to them along their poetic voyage of exploration.

He taught a course in poetry writing for LifeQuest of Arkansas. Each period began with the participants sharing what they had written since the previous session. During the latter part of each period, they reviewed a chapter from his poetry book, *Golden Thunder*. Whatever that inspired them to write, they would share during the next class, followed by the reading of another chapter. He compiled and edited the poetry produced by the class into a book entitled *LifeQuest Poets: A Journey of Discovery and Sharing*.

He may be contacted at alward@ualr.edu. His books can be ordered from WordsWorth Books (wordsworthbooks.org) by email at wordsworthbooks@sbcglobal.net and by phone at 501-663-9198.